Final Request

Final Request

At Wit's End

Life Before The Cross

Linda Lou Jones

Psalm 45:1 "... my tongue is the pen of a ready writer."

Website: www.lindaloujones.com
Other Books By Linda Lou Jones:
The Agonized Heart...No More 'Abandon Abusers'
Scalpel to Sword 'Everyone Hurts Somewhere'
Available from Amazon.com and other retailers

Soon to be Released:
Praise The Lord - 'Life After The Cross'
Rainbow Rider 'Wannabe Biker 40+ Takes Lessons'
The Rent Is Paid 'Monthly Miracles Manifested'
Blog: https://www.rightlady.blogspot.com
Follow Me On Twitter: https://www.twitter.com/rightlady7

Dedication

I dedicate this book to Jesus Christ
You became much more than a Savior to me
You are the only One, Who never let me down
No one ever cared for me like You, Jesus
You are the God of impossibilities
You are the God of the miraculous
You saved, healed, and delivered me
You did it without any fuss
Thank You Jesus for not giving up on me
And for changing me
I love You!

Linda Lou Jones

Table of Contents

Preface

JESUS LOVES ME this I know, for the Bible tells me so. He made himself real to me daily and asked me to share with you, my readers, how He revealed himself to me; whether it is in *a song, a book, or a poem.*

It began when I as a single parent reached a dead end; an end to the wide road that leads to hell. I turned to Jesus Christ for help. Three months after making the commitment to be a Christian, I had written fifty poems. In the thirty some years prior to this time, I had only written two poems. Writing is a gift God gave me and much to my surprise when I counted the poems, I suddenly heard a very clear voice say, *"Now write a book to go with each chapter."* **God.... gave me a mandate!**

It took two years to write the chapters because much healing was done as my life was being transformed. Much spiritual surgery was done on the inside, from 10 P.M. until 2 A.M. I wrote without a typewriter, longhand, shed many tears, but the job got done. My inner healing was a process that simultaneously enabled me to write the 'chapters' as pain was released and replaced with healing. Chapter sequence shows the deeper the pain the longer it took to unbury and unlock the pain.

This shows the depth of damage and fragmenting I suffered. The deeper the wound to the soul, the further one tends to bury it within, in an effort to remove the pain. To make that smooth would be to steer the truth in another direction and that would defeat the purpose of presenting truth. *What you read is from the heart of someone prior... to making the commitment to Jesus. It shows my thought process, focus, confusion, desperation, and bondage. Then I share my thoughts as I begin to change with God's help and write from my heart exactly what happened, step by step.*

Truth is what I bring to you and pray you recognize Jesus working in many ways, in my life. Whether it be to write a song, a book, a poem. Jesus is the greatest communicator in the world. He talks a lot through the Holy Spirit. Many simply fail to listen...believe... and receive. *This book will be like an arrow pointing you in the right direction and helping you to understand God's ways.*

The following is my first critique from *Rosemary, a lady who worked at Shiloh Christian Book Store in Oshawa, Ontario, Canada,* years ago. She said: **"It is so simple... it SHOULDN'T work... BUT it DOES!!!"**

CHAPTER 1

Final Request

SPRING WAS AT the door with buds sprouting forth, grass beginning to grow, flower beds blossoming, yet in my heart it was not spring at all. Just dark, nothing but black... numbness... coldness... a constant ache. *I decided what I would do.*

My parents, my daughter and I had been staying at my Aunt's house for a few days. She lived in the town where I spent the first ten years of my life; Sawyerville, Quebec, Canada. It was about five hundred miles from our current homes in Bowmanville, Ontario, Canada.

It had been years since I was able to visit with lots of these relatives. I should have been happy and excited about all the family I would be in contact with again, *but I wasn't.* Though it was great to see my Aunt, and feel the love and warmth in her huge beautiful old home, *this did nothing to soften the hardness in my heart.*

I said goodnight to my parents and my Aunt, giving an extra hug and studying their faces intently for a moment. A pain and sorrow filled me, as I realized how terribly much we loved each other. I did not want to hurt them, yet I knew what I must do. Slowly, I climbed the beautiful wood staircase to my room. It was such an effort to climb each stair, as if some force were pushing me back; trying to prevent me from retiring.

After preparing for bed, I looked in the mirror; every hair was in place, I was freshly bathed and wore a pretty new nightgown, yet my face revealed a different story. The saddest eyes looked back at me in that mirror; a reflection I shall never forget. They truly did reveal the soul and its sorrowful state. *"The eyes are the mirror to one's soul."* How very true. They revealed such an emptiness, dryness, longing and sorrow...........an oncoming death.

Lying on the bed, one hand crossed over the other, I prepared for my final request. With my lungs full of air I spoke directly from my heart. **"Dear God, I want to die**. *I do not want any more to do with this earth. I want to go to heaven and be with Jesus. You know that I love my daughter and my family so much, but* *without my son, I can't continue any longer. I know you have given me a lot, but having a son and not seeing him is too much. I know you hear me, so I'll try to explain. I am not a violent person....no guns or pills for me. A heart attack is how I will die, and I want you to do this tonight. This is the best way; quiet, though sudden, and hopefully little pain. I am ready to die now because I want to go to heaven and be with Jesus. Amen."*

My hands clutched a little Gideon Bible I had owned since I was ten years old. It comforted me, and though I had never read it much, I felt God would forgive me, somehow.

I lay with my eyes closed and felt so calm, no fear at all, just anticipation. How long before He would come and take me up to heaven? I felt like I was almost floating already. There was no pain, no hurt, a strange weightlessness surrounded me and my room was warm. This calm feeling was so beautiful I nearly dozed off until I heard a car approaching.

In my mind, I knew I would not go to heaven by CAR!! When the car was out front, the horn honked twice. I was reminded of a bumper sticker I once saw, *"Honk twice if you love Jesus."* A smile covered my peaceful face until the car passed by. Sooooo impatient was I. I started to cry. *"Please, dear Jesus, you know I've had enough. Whatever it takes to cope with things here, I'm not made of that kind of stuff."*

The next thing I knew, I had rolled over on my tummy and in my hands was the Bible just waiting to be read. There was a piece of paper in it, used as a marker. I opened it there at Revelation and began to read. I was so surprised, this was GOOD. I WANTED to read and I began to understand.

A spark had been lit deep in my heart and my whole inner being was alive and stirring emotions of all sorts. Like a kettle beginning to boil or a pot beginning to perk, I read and read and the more I read, the more I perked! This was ironic! The Bible never looked like this before, because I had not let "self" die. My heart was full of Linda. Jesus could not shine through. Now, I opened the door of my heart and asked him in, thus making Linda number two! A more sincere request I had never made.

For two hours I read, but it seemed like only minutes. Time did not mean a thing. **I was in a new world with**

the King! I was a heavenly citizen on earth. Next thing I knew there was a knock on my door. My Aunt had retired for the night and asked why my light was on so late. It WAS 2 A.M.! I did not want her to be hurt, so I did not tell her I had wanted to die. Though in total bewilderment myself, I tried to explain to her that my feelings had changed.

I asked her, "Haven't you ever seen someone that really bugs you because you know they have something you don't, yet you don't know what it is......you can't quite put your finger on it? You just know they have an answer that you have not found and this "SOMETHING" about them puts a big question mark in your mind? WELL, I'VE FOUND IT!"

My Aunt looked at me, studying my face deeply, an almost gaunt expression on her face. I did not wait for any answer, I continued. *"IT'S IN REVELATION. READ IT!"* I was so excited by now, perched up on the side of the bed. She choked up a bit and suggested I get some rest. She knew my nerves had been bad because of the stress I was under concerning my son, and was worried about me. Now, she was not just worried, but somewhat alarmed.

I turned my light out, at least I turned the bedroom light out (my pilot light was lit...AND HOW!) When I thought my Aunt was asleep I turned the light back on and read with such a hunger that again, time meant nothing. Knock, knock, knock. It was my Aunt, again!! *"What is wrong?"* she asked. *"Nothing, I'm okay.....REALLY! I just lost all track of time reading, sorry!"* Out went my light in a hurry. It WAS 5 A.M.! This time I went to sleep for sure!

I slept like a baby, and justifiably so. That is exactly what I was, a new baby in Christ. A born again Christian, spiritually born again. At that point, I had no idea the importance of the change that had taken place, the miracles Jesus had in store for me, or the many smiles he would put on my face.

When I went downstairs in the morning, the wallpaper in the den fascinated me. I did not understand why I couldn't seem to take my eyes off it. I had seen it before and it never had this effect on me. **1 Corinthians 15:51 "We shall not sleep, we shall be changed."** The paper had a green vine all over it and little did I know it would be seventeen months before I would understand what it meant spiritually. (Jesus is the vine, and we are the branches.)

John Chapter fifteen. Consequently, "Abiding In The Vine" is a favorite chorus of mine and **John 15:7 "If ye abide in me, and my words abide in you, ye shall ask what ye will, and it shall be done unto you."** is one of my favorite scripture verses.

Though I did not understand why I was so drawn to the vine on the wallpaper, one thing I knew for sure: I was inspired to try again, *I did NOT want to DIE!*

> *I picked up a pen and began to write but no words came. All I could do was draw happy faces again, and again, and again. Each one was reflecting my soul, a glance in the mirror also confirmed this. My eyes never looked like this before, so bright and they absolutely sparkled. Whatever was happening, I knew it was GOOD!*

I made this "Final Request" in May of 1976. The chain of miracles I've seen and received and experienced since then is exactly that, miraculous!

Final Request

I bid everyone goodnight
Then went upstairs to bed
With every hair in place
And my new nightgown on
I lay motionless
My face without expression
My hands folded one over the other
I took a big breath in preparation
For my "Final Request"

I confessed to God my desire to die
I wanted nothing more to do with this earth
My wish was to be in heaven with Jesus
I told Him that though I loved my daughter
My family, and friends
Without my son, I wanted it to end
Although He blessed me with so much
I could not continue my life as such
I really felt He could hear me

So, I continued to explain
Telling him I was not a violent person
No pills or guns for me
I told him a heart attack would be okay
And I wanted this to be the day!
My hands clutched my little Bible,
My most cherished possession now
Though I had not understood the bits I did read
I felt God forgave me somehow.

As I lay there waiting to float toward heaven
I could not sleep, only stare
How long before God would grant me my wish?
I felt so prepared and calm,
Wondering what it would feel like
My little trip to heaven
I almost dozed off
Until I heard a car approaching
In my mind, I knew I would not
reach heaven by car

Just as the car reached the house
The horn honked two times
I was reminded
"Honk twice if you love Jesus".

The car passed on by
I lay there and started to cry
"Please, dear Jesus, You know I've had enough
Whatever I need to cope with things here
I'm not made of that kind of stuff."

Next thing I knew I was on my tummy
My Bible in front of my eyes
A little piece of paper
Had been placed as a marker
I opened it there at Revelation
I started to read and read and read
And now I could understand
I wanted to yell and run downstairs
But couldn't waste the time

The Bible never looked like this before
But then, I had not opened the door
The door of my heart to let Jesus in
I read for two hours till my Aunt came upstairs
She inquired why my light was on so late
I did not tell her I had wanted to die
In glorious excitement,
I tried to explain
My feelings were not the same

At times in the past
There was something I envied in others
Though their number was small
It was something
I couldn't put my finger on
At all, yet I knew for sure
They had an answer I could not find
There was just something about them
That put a question in my mind.

Well now I had the answer
So, I told my Aunt
It's in Revelation,
READ IT!
She appeared a little gaunt!
I was so excited
Perched up on the side of the bed
She choked up a little bit
But insisted I retire my head.

I did, but not for long
She retired down the hall
I waited until I thought she was asleep
Then turned my light back on
Hungrily read my Bible, not making a peep

Next thing I knew
My Aunt was at the door again
Wondering what was wrong with me
It WAS 5A.M.!

This time I turned the light out
Ready for sleep
‹Without
A doubt!
When I awoke and went downstairs
Something about the wallpaper attracted me
Regardless of what else I looked at
The wallpaper was all I could see
It was paper covered with a green vine.

It was months later
Before I received spiritual understanding
Regarding me being so drawn by the vine
I learned Jesus is the vine
We are the branches, from He
One thing I knew for sure
Though I didn't really know why
I was inspired to try again
I did not want to die!

I picked up a pen
Because I wanted to write
But instead I started to draw
Happy faces, happy faces, are all I saw
That night!
May of 1976
Is when I made this "Final Request"
The chain of miracles I've seen since then
Have been the best!

CHAPTER 2

Broken Lives

MY HUSBAND AND both of my children had been gone
for six days, their whereabouts unknown to me. My
nerves were like an elastic band stretched nearly to
the breaking point. *If I ever needed to know there IS a
God, I needed to know then!* *No one else could help. My
husband could not be charged with kidnapping because
he was the father. Who could help me? Man? No. Only
God.*

In desperation, I turned to God and though I had not
gone to church for years I just knew he was listening
to my prayer. In four more days my family returned
home, but not until after I received many torturous
long-distance phone calls. The mental pressure was
such that it is only because of the grace of God that
I was able to withstand such threats. One time I was
told by my husband to say good-bye to my children
on the phone because his next step was to take them
to Europe and I would never see them again. I know

now it was God who gave me the strength I needed to cope with the situation.

My husband did return home with both of the children, but he discussed in front of the children how we would divide the furniture in our home, upon separating. I was so upset that this be discussed in front of the children; my nerves were so bad I could not think straight. I was not able to concentrate; I could not take my eyes off my children. I was so thankful they were home safe and sound.

At the peak of an argument my husband insisted he did not want to leave. He wanted us to stay together. He insisted he loved me and wanted to continue as before, as if no damage had been done at all over the past ten days when I did not know where the children were, not to mention the problems in the previous thirteen years of marriage.

I was very bitter at this time, (a forgiving spirit I did not have, nor did I know such a thing was possible to release). I did know I did not love my husband and I could no longer live in fear like I had for so many years. His suicide threats were only one way I was bound by fear for so long. The fear in me reached the point that I decided we were separating and I didn't care if he shot me because I wanted to die anyway, things were so bad. On this basis, the decision was easy.

My husband moved out after receiving a letter from my lawyer ordering him out within six days because I owned the house. He owned the business. He moved out immediately, but he took our son with him. This, I was totally unprepared for. Broken lives is one of the poems resulting from this chain of events.

The bitterness my heart was so strong, yet so was the determination to get my son back. Fear escalates and I had reached the point of 'enough is enough' so going to a lawyer was a way of removing the fear of my husband. Even though I did not believe in divorce, but I had seen the damage done to the kids as things were, as well as to myself and without any sincere attempt to reconcile my decision was easy. I faced the fear finally.

No Christian ever came to me and told me, in love, that what I was doing was against scripture, against God's will, or simply that Jesus loved me. Let alone offer to pray for me. *Silent Christians are not effective.*

They are like a light with a burned-out bulb. Just taking up space but good for nothing, spiritually.

One day a neighbor came to my home to deliver a product, she was someone that is in church every Sunday. I asked her to pray for me due to marriage breakup and she did not know how to pray. I kept waiting and bowed my head, but she could not pray. I was astounded. That fruit did not make me want to attend church. Yet, since both my husband and I did not serve God, what were the options? Serve self or the devil, it was both.

Yet we believed in Jesus Christ. Well so does the devil. Our rewards were spiritual death, broken lives; and that was only the beginning, not the end! Honestly, if you asked us if we were Christians we would have said yes, because we believed we were. Being a believer is not the same as applying what the Bible teaches and we could not do that because to us, the Bible was a closed book. It was not ever read by us, nor did we pray. Do things your way, means you pay. My husband was involved in a lot more sin than I realized at the time. When the truth finally surfaced I understood why his obsession with guns and the fear he projected onto others.

It came from within him because he feared his sin would be exposed and would rather die than go to prison. Me getting a divorce was a blessing in disguise though I was blind to the reason at that time, unfortunately. Broken lives was the result of a home without a solid foundation, lives were shattered because self was number one. My attempts to reach God seemed futile and as I became more desperate I did what I could to stop the fear. See a lawyer. My love for my kids was stronger than the fear so I got motivated. *Lives were broken before the divorce, not because of the divorce. Fact.*

Broken Lives

Destiny, fate, justice, pure hell,
What kind of world is this I live in
Shattered heart and hopes, broken dreams
A never-ending nightmare
Yet, something within me drives on
Like a tiny spark in a fire
That refuses to burn out
In my desperation, I turn to God again and again
Yet more troubles surround me
And tears fall like rain
How much suffering can one person endure
More importantly, why, what reason for such pain
It is so difficult to start again
My blessings are many; loved ones, friends, a home
Yet one burden severely unbalances the scales
My precious son has been taken away
I know not if or when I'll see him again someday
He's alive, yet he's dead
For he has no voice in the matter

A child like a shadow
Who feels his duty is to follow
A man who is heartless, ruthless and sallow
Will he find the strength
To do what is right
God knows I've tried everything
With all my might
It is not fair the pain
He has had to endure
I pray he finds courage
And faith for sure

CHAPTER 3

Loneliness

THREE MONTHS PASSED and I saw my son... but a few minutes at a time. His father would not let him come and visit his sister and me. We rarely had a chance to be alone with my son, so it was difficult for anything fruitful to evolve from any unexpected encounter with him on the street. Because he was afraid his father would get mad if he saw him talking to us.

He was in the same kind of bondage of fear I had lived in for so many years. It broke my heart to see and realize this. If it took me thirteen years to break away from this situation, how long would it take him?

As far as lawyers, court, etc. were concerned, the red tape was incredible. I had visitation rights, but my husband would not let my daughter or I see my son, unless we were visiting him as well. When we did visit on two occasions the conversation was so strained and unnatural the tension was incredible.

I felt more harm than good was done because my husband kept insisting he loved me and made me look like big bad mommy responsible for making him move… breaking up the marriage, etc. because I would not respond to his request.

Yet if I renewed the relationship it would not be the best thing. The children were being hurt in the atmosphere they had been living in, so I tried to be strong; though when we left after a visit my insides literally felt torn out inch by inch. We did visit my son and husband at their apartment twice and I saw my son's eyes fill with tears when we embraced, and my daughter's, as well. It was a living hell for each of us. My son was eleven and a half years old and my daughter just turning eight years old.

The hurt was so deep for all of us it is almost impossible for someone that has not experienced a broken home to realize how tragic a marriage breakdown is. The bitterness that welled up inside was like a mountain about to explode until God blessed me with a gift. He gave me the gift of writing poetry and it was a form of therapy for me because the poetry provided an outlet for all of the suppressed anger, bitterness and hurt. At that time, I did not realize the gift was from God, consequently I did not give Him the glory.

The loneliness enveloped me like a prison. No husband, no son, after so many years were a big adjustment for me and for my young daughter. Like so many other wives from broken marriages, I quickly learned who my real friends were.

Most marriages of my so-called friends were so insecure that the wives thought of me not as a friend any longer, but as bait for their husbands. Consequently, socializing with others was nearly completely eliminated except for a few true friends that had their heart in the right place.

Without my parents support at that time I could not have endured the things I went through, because I did not know Jesus as Lord of my life, so I did not know how to lean on Him. My parents supported me faithfully, yet they were hurting deeply also because of not being able to see their grandson that they love so dearly. They encouraged me when I was down, my father played a double role in my daughter's life; that of father and grandfather, and did it expertly.

I am so thankful he has always had a great love for children and knew exactly what my daughter needed and when. My brother also became even more important to her, as a father image, although she did not see him as often. I learned to value the relationship between my brother and myself more, and felt a stronger bond between us each time I saw him. He is the only brother I have, so without any sisters, or husband and son, he has become an irreplaceable person in my life. I love him so much, and since he is a trucker, (owner/operator Buffalo Bob) he also knows what loneliness is. Sometimes it is not until a family breaks up that people realize how much they really mean to each other.

Prior to the break-up of my marriage, family counseling, three different psychiatrists, and our family doctor all did not mend any broken lives because they were trying to help us in man's way with man at the head, not God. God's way is successful, and far different from the ways of the world. He is the greatest psychiatrist, marriage counselor, family counselor, and friend you could ever have! With God all things are possible.

My husband and I had taken steps to save our marriage for a period of one year, through counseling. We hadn't simply walked out without at least some effort to mend our marriage. Because of this, I felt no guilt because I knew I had done all I could. I learned I did not love him; the love had gradually been smothered by fear and jealousy. Consequently, I decided I could no longer live with him.

When my husband left the pressure left because the fear was gone, but a new pressure took root because of not having my son with me. Some people were of the opinion that for us to stay together thirteen years we must have had something going for us. This is true. We had fear binding us together (and I was under bondage in many other ways which I did not understand at that time) and this is not a healthy relationship for anyone. I knew what I lived and how I felt and I know when I smiled I did not smile from inside out. My smile was a mask, without a doubt.

The spirit of fear is capable of putting a person in such bondage. I will not elaborate in any way other than what has been revealed previously because it is not my intention to point the finger at anyone because I have made many mistakes too. I have been able to fully forgive my husband for everything and I pray for his salvation. I know that through Christ, God has forgiven my mistakes, my sins. Only Christ could set me free, and only through Christ was it possible for me to completely forgive.

The new type of pressure that entered my life when my husband would not let my son visit my daughter and I, was too much for me to endure. For at least a few months I had a pity party. Poor me, poor, poor me…that is all I could think.

I was so worried, uptight, depressed, could not eat, smoked heavily, could not sleep, and had night-mares as well. Once I dreamt all the diamonds fell out of my wedding rings, and the second time I dreamt I was being strangled. A third dream was that I was being drowned, and a fourth dream was that our killer trained German shepherd guard dog was commanded to attack me. **I lived a life of living hell on earth when I was awake, and when I was asleep. Peace was foreign to me.**

I remember looking at my Christmas card list just two months before, (we separated in February) and now the big majority of the names were just that, NAMES. Where were all these well-meaning friends and neigh-bors now? *This was the most difficult time of my life and they did not even phone. They did not want to get involved.*

Yet, when the police came to check if I had heard from my husband or the children, their marked car could easily be seen in the driveway, more than once during that ten-day period.

Getting involved beyond this degree probably would have made them feel like they were intruding, so I remained in the house with my daughter thoroughly wrapped up in my problems. Coping with the adjustments of not seeing her father and brother was a major task for my daughter, not to mention the necessary adjustments for myself.

Pressure increased because of not having enough money to make the mortgage payment on the house, not enough groceries, cold winter weather with lots of snow, hour after hour of depressing foolish television programs, and loneliness that seemed to seep in through the walls to the pores of my skin.

The evenings were the worse time for me. I had always been interested in astrology, so now that I had so much time to read I went to the library and read every book I could find on astrology, palm reading, tea cup reading, (Yes, it went so far that I tried reading tea cups, books on numerology, plus books teaching how to read and chart horoscopes.) ALL of these topics and books I read are part of the occult - Satanic - to put it bluntly: I served Satan every time I read from these books and allowed him to fill my mind with more of his evil ways.

> **Jeremiah 10:1-5 Living Bible (TLB) "Hear the word of the Lord, O Israel: Don't act like the people who make horoscopes and try to read their fate and future in the stars! Don't be frightened by predictions such as theirs, for it is all a pack of lies. Their ways are futile and foolish. They cut down a tree and carve an idol, and decorate it with gold and silver and fasten it securely in place with hammer and nails, so that it won't fall over, and there stands their god like a helpless scarecrow in a garden! It cannot speak, and it must be carried, for it cannot walk. Don't be afraid of such a god for it can neither harm nor help, nor do you any good."**

I went to a spiritualist and had my fortune told. She did not like those words being used, "fortune told". She preferred anyone to say when phoning for an appointment; "I would like to book an appointment for a reading." She did tell me things from my past that were true, because Satan can reveal this to her, thus enticing me to return and hear more.

There was one occasion when this spiritualist gave me a picture of Jesus. Not only did the picture of Jesus hang on the wall, there was a statue of Buddha on a table with prayer requests folded and resting on one knee.

Talk about idols, and confusion, this was the limit, yet my eyes were not opened to the seriousness of what I was letting myself in for by going to this woman's home. She was wishing the construction of a particular new building was complete so I could begin learning how to do readings, since I was not employed at that time.

Oh, she was very co-operative, but you cannot serve God with one hand and Satan with the other and expect to go to heaven when your time on earth is done! **Matthew 6:24 "No man can serve two masters: for either he will hate the one, and love the other; or else he will hold to the one, and despise the other. Ye cannot serve God and mammon."**

If only I had stopped allowing Satan to blind my eyes to the facts. Anyone with any common sense at all would know this is wrong because the money never touches hands. The money is set in a container or dish in the room where the reading is done. No cash register, no receipt, no office rented, yet people were lined up in her living-room waiting for an appointment. I wonder how much of the income was reported as income, for income tax purposes. On second thought, it does not matter that I know, because for sure God knows!

Some of the things she told me worried me, not then, but a lot later. One example is when she described a particular family that was moving and said the only child was going to get lost because of making a wrong turn in a new neighborhood. This was only one way in which a seed was planted causing me to worry; yet, because I was told many good things I thought I was dwelling on them and had overlooked the negative statements.

Never did I even imagine the damage these sessions did to me. Even worse, I encouraged others to go as well and one woman was told her mother had cancer. Curiosity has resulted in a lot more damage than "killing a cat" as the old saying goes.

I had my cards read and my horoscope charted. *The more I was told, the more I believed because I was searching but I did not know what for.* After a lot of tears there came a point when I realized this kind of day to day existence had to end because it was exactly that, an existence. I was not living; and knew my life could not continue like this much longer. **This was a turning point for me because I began to face reality, not duck it.**

I asked God to help me although at the time I was not sure if He would. My outlook changed because I began to see through God's eyes though I was not aware that this… is what had happened.

Previously, when I saw the grass growing quickly, the thought of having to do all that work mowing the lawns was depressing. Now, I saw that after a rain the grass had grown so much that I bent down, ran my hand over each blade in one small patch and was in awe over the way that each blade grows so straight and green and stands so proud.

This had to be God's work. Never again did mowing the lawn give me a heavy feeling, I looked forward to it.

Even though I was still walking on earth it made me feel closer to heaven because I saw God's hand in creation.

I began to appreciate the love and joy my daughter had to offer and I strove to help her as best I could with her tremendous adjustment, a double trage- dy for her, since she did not see her daddy or her brother. She was just turning eight years old; her brother was eleven and a half. I realized although there were valleys I did have a lot of things going for me. A lot of women would have been delighted to have their own home on one acre of land with an in-ground heated pool to enjoy and share with oth- ers. So that is what I did. I shared.

Instead of self-pity, I reached out to help others and this helped me too. Instead of waiting for the phone to ring I decided it was time I did the dialing and reached out to someone.

I tried to make friends with others, call someone who might be lonely, do a good deed, etc. In no time at all with this attitude I was feeling much better and so was my daughter. Soon I had a pool full of friends enjoying a swim on a hot summer day, and they did not take advantage of me. They often brought the dinner with them to barbeque when we got together and shared. It was a two-way street. They enjoyed using the pool and I enjoyed their company. Come to think of it, it's possible they enjoyed my company too, I'm not perfect, but I'm not ALL bad either.

Once the neighbors even got the clippers out and trimmed all the shrubs around the pool while waiting for the sun to dry them off, and once even mowed all the lawns of which there was close to an acre.

The more I reached out to help others the more I was blessed. There was no way I could out do the Lord, although I still did not know it was Him working in my life, for sure. I thought all these good things happening were just coincidences.

Soon there was no time left for loneliness, I was so busy thinking and following through ways in which to share what I had gained over the years.

Loneliness

You can't see it or hear it
But you can feel it envelop you like a prison
Four walls without windows
But, if your eyes are open
There is a door
Push forward gently
But with determination
Because it will open
When it does
You may still be alone
But you won't be lonely
Only you can overcome the loneliness
Reach out more
Make friends, call another who is lonely
Do a good deed
Instead of indulging in self-pity
Extend a helping hand to others
Smile and set goals
Your efforts will be rewarded

When you see another's face
change from desperation
To a smile of warmth and appreciation
No cost is involved
Just time on your part
You will feel the satisfaction
In your heart
Soon your days will be filled
With hours of pleasure
Hardly any time left for leisure
Or was it
Loneliness?

CHAPTER 4

You Don't Miss Him 'Till He's Gone

MY SON HOPPED on a school bus each morning, lunch box in one hand and sometimes books in the other. Reading, writing and arithmetic he was taught, the golden rule was also taught at this school.

He never objected going to school though he liked baseball better than math. Around four o'clock he would return home, plop down a book, coat, and the same old question, **"Hi Mommy, what have you got to eat?"** He never came home upset or in a turmoil. He took things in his stride, was easygoing and quiet.

He and his sister would play or watch television. He swam like a fish so he was happier when summer arrived so he could swim and scuba dive. He came to me with questions; our talks became so dear and precious to me. As time passed he continually confided in me. Our relationship is something I was proud of. I could see him learning and growing so fast. He did not hesitate to ask me questions. There was no fear.

This made me very happy because he would receive direct answers from me, not evasive or false answers as some parents give. I was determined he would get the facts at home on certain topics, in an effort to protect him from any misunderstanding or deception from others at some point.

I remember when he threw a baseball and it was a hit......a window in the house! Learning to write, to swim, to climb trees, to use a hammer and saw, picking worms, walking in puddles with his bare feet, making popcorn, playing cards and games, selling candies for the school, helping mow the lawn, catching or trying to catch butterflies with a large fish net, shoveling snow, making snowmen in the front yard, and much, much more.

Best of all I remember every night how he said his prayers: *"Now I lay me down to sleep, I pray the Lord my soul to keep. If I should die, before I wake, I pray the Lord my soul to take. God bless Mommy and Daddy and sister and make me a good boy. Amen."*

He and his sister went to Sunday school regularly for nearly two years, though their father and I did not attend church. Little did I realize then the importance those Sunday morning lessons would play in my children's lives as seeds were sown.

Then circumstances changed and my mischievous son with a dimple in his chin was taken away by his father. My heart broke in pieces. While the lawyers had their instructions, and began to battle it out my husband and son were living in town and I lived on the same road, only in the rural area. Rather than have my son change schools in February he was sent back and forth in a taxi to school.

First, my daughter would get the big yellow bus to school and frantically wave to me as it continued on down the road. Then I ran to the side door of the house and watched for the taxi to come with my son. I saw the car approaching and ran to the kitchen window, pulled back the curtains and it became my turn to wave frantically. I strained so hard to see his face, and what I saw instead was five little fingers waving, just a little wiggle from each one, but he did it for me. In just seconds the car was gone out of sight.

I would literally collapse on the floor in a flood of tears as the hurt tore through me. I died so many times, yet I was still alive. Even though it hurt so much, I knew my son needed that contact with me as much as I did with him, to strengthen and encourage him so I was determined not to miss his wave. Only God knew when I could see him again other than these flash contacts.

In the afternoon, I watched the clock carefully and waited for his return. He came, he waved, he was gone. I waited, I waved, I died, I cried, I ached, I got angry, I hurt, I wiped away the tears and waited for my daughter who would arrive soon. *So thankful was I to have her love and companionship to look forward to.*

Though there were times she and her brother had argued, they loved each other a lot. Now, many, many times she filled her pillow with tears as she longed for her brother. **No one could replace him, never, never, never! He was and still is the apple of our eye. The house was so empty without him.**

Once, when I had not seen him for months, he drove his mini bike through a field next door and when I looked out the window he was just sitting on the bike waiting for me to come. He waved with his arm way up in the air, and then left with his friends and their bikes on the trail. That moment I will never forget. I was so moved, so touched, yet it was like a knife going through me as the hurt spread from head to toe. I wanted to talk to him so badly, but he knew if his father found out he even talked to me he would get very angry with him, so *my son did all he could, he waved.*

When it was his birthday four months after we had been separated, his dad brought him to visit for a few minutes. This was his twelfth birthday and my daughter and I gave him a little white Bible, the New Testament, and a gold cross on a chain.

I still believed in God even though I was not receiving spiritual food from church since I did not attend; and I still believed that someday my son would be with me, and that God knew about all the hurt.

When my son arrived for this brief visit, his embrace was like gold. His eyes filled with tears as he hugged me. My heart they did hold. How very true; you don't miss him until he's gone.

You Don't Miss Him 'Till He's Gone

He got the bus each morning
Ready for another day at school
Reading, writing, arithmetic
Learning the Golden Rule
At four o'clock the bus would return
Back home again
Still with a smile
Whether sunshine or rain
Plop down a book
Or a baseball bat
There goes his coat
And his hat
Hi Mommy
What have you got to eat
A sandwich or an apple
Tasted like a treat
He played with his sister

Or watched T.V.
I always knew
Where he would be
He was very bright
And quick to learn
Swam like a fish
Knowledge he did yearn
We became very close
Our talks were sincere
He was a very good boy
And to me very dear
Then circumstances changed
A separation I had
He was taken from me
By his dad
No more smile
From a dimpled chin
My mischievous boy gone
Lord, how I missed him
My heart broke in pieces
It was hard for him too
But he felt obeying his dad
Was the thing to do
He was sent to school
In a taxi, each day

Five fingers waved in the window
What a price to pay
Phone conversations were strained
My heart broke again
He was being turned against his mom
By a man who was deranged
Would this pain ever end
The days were so long
I needed my son
Who was so strong
His sister missed him dearly
She loved him so much
They argued at times
But love is such
She filled her pillow
With wet little tears
Longing for a boy
Close to her in years
He was the apple of our eye
No one could replace
The house was so empty
Without his grace
He touched my heart
When he sat on his bike
Waited for me to wave

Then off like a light
One day I saw him
His embrace was like gold
His eyes filled with tears
My heart they did hold

CHAPTER 5

Breakdown

MY EYES JUST would not close. My mind would not shut down. As thoughts raced in my head my body became more and more exhausted. Five days and nights passed and I had not slept at all. As I delved deeper and deeper into the occult, satan got a tighter grip on my life. He was leading me down the wide road to hell and I did not pull back. **My intention was to study psychology, but 'O' is next to 'P' and I got sidetracked at the library by 'O' occult.**

Soon I tried reading tea leaves and cards. I spent hours on end studying astrology and was determined to compile charts for others. The library was one place I visited often and read books on palm reading, e.s.p. Transcendental meditation, spiritualist mediums, etc.

Since I had so many hours each day with little to do, and an enormous void to fill, I tried to fill the void with a wealth of knowledge from books. **Little did I realize I**

was polluting my mind with Satan's food and the more I read and delved into the occult, the more depressed and despondent I became. Yet, I continued to keep busy in this way because without my son I could not face each day unless there was some way to busy my mind.

Worse came to worse and soon Satan had picked at my mind more incessantly than birds picking away at a fresh red strawberry. I was gradually losing control, my mind became very inhabited by satanic thoughts and an obsession to delve deeper and deeper into the occult. Also, the enemy was suggesting I do things that were detrimental to my health. I did not realize how quickly I was sinking. I thought I was thinking these thoughts at the time, but now I know it was but one way the devil lures people toward his ultimate destination, hell!

One week-end my parents were going to Quebec to visit relatives and did not want to leave me alone. They took me with them and immediately after our return home, I phoned the police and they came to talk to me. In my mind, I believed a bizarre story about others, which, had it been true; would have sent them to prison. (I won't recount it because it would glorify satan).

After my parents explained my marital situation to the police and I told them I wanted to go to the local hospital, they understood and agreed to take me. **When one officer started to get into my dad's car with me I became terrified because he was wearing a gun and I would not stay in the car unless he took it off.**

He took it out of his holster and handed it to his partner who was driving the police car. *I shook like a leaf as I watched the gun being exchanged from one officer to another. They did not know the reason for my fear of guns, but God knows and I know, and it is justified.*

Once the gun was out of sight I began to calm down and upon arrival at the hospital, I told the doctor I had not slept, was not on any drugs, was under tremendous stress because of not seeing my son, and that I was hallucinating. This final statement surprised him.

I looked at the big clock on the wall and the hands were turning clockwise full speed ahead, very, very quickly. I knew, in reality, this could not be happening, so I told the doctor what my eyes saw and asked him to help me.

He prescribed what he thought was best: pills, pills, pills, sleep, sleep, sleep, eat, eat, and eat. For ten days, this is all I did, except for the times I was awake and bound by fear.

Because of my husband's growing interest in guns over the years, and his suicidal tendencies as well as threats to me, I developed an enormous fear of guns.

The worst incident was when I had been in the basement doing laundry, came upstairs to the kitchen and as I entered saw my husband loading his magnum. He was sitting down near the wall phone. I stopped in my tracks, watched him load the gun, cock the loaded gun, opened his mouth and aim the gun into his mouth (after first aiming it at... then past me). Something inside of me snapped.

I heard a scream, did not realize it came out of me as I turned to exit by the back door not knowing if he would come after me, shoot me in the back, or my head; while I also listened to know if he shot himself like he always threatened to do. My feet stopped, I blanked out, don't remember entering the house again but I remember thinking we were not even arguing and he was acting like this. What was happening inside his head? I did not have that answer for years, but I do remember that it was a long time before I could look at a television program with guns because of the damage this did to me.

Although he did not pull the trigger I envisioned the results had he done so and suffered for years after because of the intense grip fear had on me. This experience was one of the ways in which mental cruelty over a period of years resulted in my failing health, until I reached the point of a nervous breakdown and was hospitalized for manic depression to receive help. I admitted myself to the local hospital and was there ten days.

During the time, I was in the hospital there was one thing I would not let go of. *It was my little Gideon Bible I received when I was in grade five at ten years of age.* Though I did not read it much, I carried it all the time as I walked up and down the halls. When I slept it was under my pillow or in my hand. **I got strength from the closeness of that Bible that I couldn't get elsewhere.**

Once at three in the morning I asked the nurse if there was a minister somewhere in the hospital that I could talk to because I needed to talk and couldn't sleep anyway. There was, and he just happened to be on the same floor as me, and he also just happened to be sitting in the lobby reading his Bible at that very moment! Although he was a patient, and it was three A.M.!

(This is in no way a coincidence; this is what I call a "God instance"; a perfect example of how God puts the right people together in the right place at the right time for a Godly purpose. He ordained this meeting.)

With me in the hospital it was necessary for my mother to care for my daughter and drive her to and from school. When my husband discovered I was in the hospital he went to her school and took her out of class (much to the chagrin of the principal/teacher and her classmates) one day. He then enrolled her in another school in town.

My mother could do nothing about this and I did not know he had taken her when he came to the hospital. All I saw was he and both children standing beside my bed looking down at me. My husband did not have to say anything, he was gloating. When I felt the full impact of the fact that my daughter was with him too, I completely gave up.

I felt I had lost the only thing I had left to fight for it was terrible enough without my son living with me, but; now with my daughter gone too I wanted to die. **The spark went out and I WANTED to die more than at any time in my life! There wasn't an ounce of strength left in my body. My eyes blinked, but the rest of my body was completely listless.**

I did not even think about food or water, day or night, life or death, I just wanted the blackness to envelop me and let it be done with, but that did not happen. I would think as I lay there, "It is finished, it is over, it is done, I'll die now, this is it, my life is over but it is okay because I want to die, I am going to die. Hell is what I have been living. Now I will have peace, rest, quiet, no more thoughts, no more worry, no more hurt, no more pain, no more crying, no more heartbreak, I'll just die."

My son stood near the foot of the bed and patted my leg and stood with the most sympathetic, yet loving expression on his face as he looked at me. I knew he was upset and did not understand what was wrong with me and at the same time I wondered what he had been told about my condition.

I did have some pride and did not want him being told I was crazy, and I was concerned about both children worrying about me. *I KNEW I would live (even though I didn't want to) but did THEY?* I was in a local hospital in my hometown as opposed to being in a psychiatric ward, but this was not of much comfort to them at their ages.

My heart was torn in shreds when I saw my husband gloating as he stood with both kids about to leave. It was more than I could bear. My daughter cried and so did I. I was so heavily sedated I could not get up. *They left, as did my hope.* I wanted to throw the plant my husband brought out the window, but I had no strength. I just wanted to die, right then and there!

My family doctor knew us for years and I believe God used him in a very important way. He came into the room, took one look at me and looked me directly in the eye as he bent closer while at the same time squeezing my arm and said: **"Don't let him GET to you!"**

I looked back at the doctor and saw how serious he was and suddenly I thought: *"He's right. I won't give up. I'm not a quitter. I love my kids and I'll fight for them because I know they love me and I know I am best for them"*

> *It was at this moment the spark was lit. I had a new determination to survive and I immediately set a goal. We are all given a free will and I exercised mine by choosing to live and there was a purpose in my life now. The clock had been started once again. It is no secret what God can do!*

This does not mean it was a smooth road from here on in. As I lay in bed that night in the hospital satan attacked my mind worse than ever. He attacked my newfound determination with the spirit of fear.

He told me the noise I heard was a bomb ticking inside the plant my husband brought. This may sound funny to read, but I lived in such fear I actually tried not to breathe for fear of shaking the bed and somehow jarring the "bomb" to set it off. This was a reality in my mind.

I tried not to move a muscle, but I shook because of the fear and couldn't control the shaking. I heard noises and thought it might be the foil around the plant pot, but it wasn't. The devil kept picking at my mind like the vulture and the robber he is until I was convinced there was a bomb in the plant pot.

The combined fear of a bomb in my room and a feeling of claustrophobia caused by the fact that the side rails on my bed were raised up, were too much. I literally dove to the foot of my bed until I hit the floor, and then ran hysterically down the corridor to the nurses' station.

(As I think back I wonder who was more frightened for a moment, me or the nurse that I ran into when rounding a corner in the corridor.) I heard what seemed to be my thoughts saying, "The nurses will think you are crazy for sure. They'll just laugh at you and put you right back in the same bed beside the same plant that is still ticking. They will. Wait and see. Patients have to stay in bed and they will put you right back in bed." **(I know now those were not my thoughts, that were a way in which the devil attacks our mind with a tormenting spirit.)**

I thank God the nurse was cool, calm, and collected. She patiently waited until I was coherent and showed the love I desperately needed by simply holding my hand and putting one arm around my shoulders. I sensed she really cared what happened to me, yet at the same time I could not understand why she wasn't running in the opposite direction in an effort to be safe from the bomb.

I insisted the nurse throw the plant out the window to save the other patients. (No offense to the neighbors, who lived outside, I was thinking with a very broad scope at that time.) I even opened the hall window but she put the plant in the storage room and still seemed very calm about it all. Needless to say, I did not go near the storage room!

There was no bomb, only the devastating fear of one and the plant was never returned to my room at my adamant request. The nurse did manage to get me back to bed after bringing me tea and talking to me until I went to sleep.

There were three other women in the same room I was in and a few nights later fear struck again. The woman next to my bed was a very elderly, very frail woman who was strapped into a childlike harness each night at bedtime to prevent her from falling out of bed or sitting up.

One night she awoke and very quietly undid the harness, sat up, rocked and jiggled her bed to move it where she wanted it to be. She achieved her goal. Parked next to my bed as I slept.

I was awakened suddenly and when I opened my eyes there was a face staring at mine, just inches away and it was the most wrinkled shadow filled face of this very elderly woman who was sitting up on the side of her bed smiling (without her dentures) at me! I couldn't even scream at first, and then one scream came out from deep within.

Staff came immediately and she was back on her own half of the room fast. This was enough to scare some-one who has NOT had a nervous breakdown so you can imagine how it affected me. I absolutely refused to sleep in that room and since the rooms were full, I slept on a stretcher in the hall with a room divider around me for three days, much to my relief.

I remember waking up one morning with hot tears pouring forth. The nurse came by and patted my arm in a consoling gesture. This brought forth more tears. *(It is true that body language speaks louder than words and more effectively sometimes.)* **I told her I just wanted her to**

stay a minute because I needed to know SOMEONE cared about me. She did. She was there. That was all I needed. My need for that moment was met and I received the help I needed. (Thank God for competent nurses.)

During my hospitalization period my mother was so faithful and helpful. Though she was very upset about my health and my children, she kept her chin up and I drew strength and courage from her. There were two girlfriends that visited me also, and this was the moment in which I realized how extremely important it is to take time to visit the sick because it certainly meant more to me than I can say. It showed love.

You don't have to say a word either. Just be there. You never realize how important this is until you are a patient. If you are fortunate enough not to have ever been a patient, please take my advice to heart because it is true. I know. I lived it and experience is a great teacher.

At one point my pride got in the way. I became very concerned about what people would say about me. I was not a celebrity, but my husband and I did own a variety store; so we worked long hours daily with the public and although they did not necessarily know our name they knew who we were.

I wondered what their reaction would be. Would they think I was crazy? What would they say about me? Would any of them come and visit me? How could I ever face them if they think I am crazy? I had no idea what to expect.

Then, while walking down the corridor to put my time in I overheard some nurses talking and looking at me. The voices followed as I continued walking.... "That's a shame, and she is so pretty." "Yea, and so young, it's too bad." *(I can tell you pity is NOT what someone in my condition needed. I did not need someone acting like "it's all over." I needed someone to encourage me to "Press on.")*

One morning I saw reality and grasped hold of it. I knew in my heart I had done everything I could to save my marriage. I had given it my all. Consequently, there was no guilt. I also knew many others would have been hospitalized long before I was if they had experienced what I did, so I tried not to let any comments from others that weren't edifying bother me. *I knew everyone has a breaking point and I had reached mine. You know when you have done your best, and I knew I had.*

The following is a note I wrote on a card for my parents and grand-parents who were visiting while I was in the hospital. In retrospect, I believe strongly God was speaking strongly through me, revealing truths to them and to me as I wrote, although at the time I was totally unaware of this. The note said:

"May 14, 1976. Hi Mom, Dad, Gram & Grandpa Charles,

The donuts, powder, perfume and nighties were a real pick-me-up! I know I look good outside so now I'm just trying to feel better inside and I know I will, just a little time and patience. Have three friendly talkative room-mates so it helps a lot. Don't worry about me, I hung in there this long and certainly don't expect to quit now. Happiness is the result of your own striving.

Linda.

Happiness seemed a long distance away at that time, like a light at the far end of a tunnel. Nevertheless, I had the determination I needed to get well and I did. After ten long days passed I was able to leave the hospital and went to live with my parents for a few weeks, then I returned to my own home alone.

Each day that passed my longing to see my children continued to increase. I was determined my daughter was not going to stay at the apartment with my husband and son. She was going to live with me. I had returned to my own home to live and the silence was unbearable.

I phoned the store and to my surprise my husband agreed to let my son, but not my daughter, come and have supper with me, but I had to have him back at the store at a set hour. Even though he wouldn't let me have my daughter there for supper too, I was thrilled at the thought of seeing my son because this was the first time he was allowed to come to the house alone.

I cooked his favorite dinner and we talked but he was very quiet. He was doing a lot of deep thinking and I could not read his mind. I knew he had been deeply hurt but I also knew my love for him was very real and I was determined to try to get him to make a decision to live with me.

I looked into his face as he sat on the countertop, over the dishwasher. He kept saying he did not know where he wanted to live or who he wanted to live with. Then he said if he lived with me it wouldn't be fair because there would be no one with his dad. The next statement he made nearly floored me. He told me that his dad told him that he had cancer of the throat.

At this point I knew I was fighting a losing battle. My son started to cry and I held him in my arms and re-signed myself to the fact that I would be driving him to the apartment to live with his father because I did understand his sense of loyalty to his dad.

With a broken heart, (because I knew this statement about cancer was a lie, yet I knew if I told my son that he would think I was just saying that so he would come and live with me) I went to my room and brought out a gift for him.

It was a coin bank in the shape of a **Royal Canadian Mounted Police Officer** in full uniform. I gave it to him with the following instructions: *"Whenever you look at this bank, whether you put money in it or not,*

I want you to remember to always be honest. These officers stand for exactly that, HONESTY, and I have taught you to be honest and I don't want you to ever forget it. Always be honest because if you aren't, it will be sure to catch up with you sooner or later. **Please remember what I am saying because it is very important son. BE HONEST ALWAYS."**

> *He looked at the bank as I handed it to him and wore a big smile. He didn't have to say anything, his eyes said it all. He received my message loud and clear and I knew he would never forget it. At that point, I somehow felt that if I had never taught him anything else, I did teach him to be honest and I knew that was a big lesson to learn and an important one.*

So I felt that although I would be driving him to his dad's I did have a degree of success with him in the short time we were together. I really needed that consolation at the time and God knew that too.

With a heavy heart, I drove him back to the store and his embrace was not to be forgotten. My daughter was outside at the front of the store and I told my son to tell her to come to the car after he crossed the road.

He did, then waved to me and continued on into the store carrying his bank. His dad was raking up papers at the front of the store and looked up, but continued raking.

My father was in his truck a few car lengths behind me at this point because he knew what I was about to do and was determined there would be no violence. **I had more than one guardian angel, to be sure.**

My daughter came to the driver's side of the car thinking I had called her over to give her a kiss and I said, *"Go around and get in the car."* She looked surprised and did exactly that. She had not seen my father parked nearby. When she sat in the front seat I saw my husband look up and stop raking and I started to shake. I didn't know if I would be able to get that car out of there or not I shook so badly. I looked at her and said, **"Do you want to live with me?"** She said, **"Yes."** I said, **"Okay, put your seat belt on, we are going to Grammies right now."** She did!

I put the car in drive and headed out kicking up a few stones at the same time. The second car I met was a police car and I was sure the driver would follow me because I was not about to waste any time. I checked the rear-view mirror constantly thinking my husband would follow me in his car and I was sure he would try to force me off the road.

I had visions of this happening as I drove through town and it's a good thing the light was green; then I was out of town after only about a mile. I took a short cut to my mothers, which meant traveling on a gravel road with lots of pot holes and the dust really flew behind me. I approached one intersection wondering if my husband would meet me at the corner because he could have taken yet another route. He wasn't there so I continued on, just a hiking it until I got to my mother's home.

The garage door was open and she stood to the side (smart woman) while I drove in. She shut the door and that was the end of a rough road in more ways than one.

She was so disappointed that my son was not with me too, but tried to keep her chin up. She was really a sensible woman and did not get easily flustered at any time. (It was a while yet before my father arrived because he had to wait for the dust to settle!) I hadn't even thought about that!

The realization of this was very painful as roots were being torn from my heart. My parents comforted my daughter, and I threw myself on the bed and cried uncontrollably. Then I tried to pull myself together once more and with a beautiful daughter to love and care for I decided to do my best to help her because I knew she was hurting too. After a few days, we returned to my home and she enrolled once again in her regular school.

I received a phone call from my son asking why I kidnapped his sister and tried my best to explain that she had agreed to come and live with me, but he could not see it that way and voiced his opinion with cutting words and much anger. I wondered when this nightmare would end, if ever.

Another step was taken in the right direction when I picked up my daughter because ***I stopped running from my husband. My desire to have her with me was stronger than the fear of him.***

The nervous breakdown was over and I was much stronger and getting stronger day by day. Having a nervous breakdown is an experience unique to itself. Each person's experiences are different, yet it is a living hell each person suffers.

Love brought me to my feet. The love my family and friends gave me and the love shown by the hospital staff was what I needed. God saw that I received it. *Love breaks through all barriers, even a breakdown!*

Breakdown

Time mattered not at all
There was no difference between day and night
The clock could have stood still for all I cared
Everything was wrong, nothing seemed right

To fill the lonely hours
I read and read and read
But it was the devil's occult food
That filled my head

The more I exposed myself to his teaching
The more in bondage I became as I
More widely opened the door
Until I could not sleep at all I was so wound up
Yet I continued to read even more

The hospital was a welcome sight
Because I knew someone would help me

It was my home for ten long days
Many new experiences were awaiting me

Fear, terror, hysteria, suicidal thoughts,
Devastation and sorrow
I lived it all while I was there
My will to die was changed
When I met a doctor that did care

He spoke the exact words I needed to hear
A new determination to fight and press on
Began when I set a goal
And my desire to die was gone

From guns to bombs
From two children to none
I was now determined to achieve my goal
My family numbered more than ONE

I prayed asking God to help me
Many times, I reached out
But I was not able to fight off satan's attacks
Of this, there was no doubt

I was in God's army without any armor
A dangerous way to be

Ephesians chapter six explains what I needed
Without any armor, the devil had the victory

I was a walking target for him
He attacked my mind
There isn't much of a battle
When one enters defenseless
A safe corner I could not find

God looked at my heart though
And heard its' sincere cry
He was with me in the valley
And faithfully encouraged me to try

God is love
It was love that brought me to my feet
Love from people God put on my path
Because of their love, there was NO defeat

Love breaks through all barriers
Love breaks through all walls
God's love lifted me victoriously
Because He answered my many calls

CHAPTER 6

The Gold Slipper

No LONGER COULD I stifle and smother the tears and hurt that welled up inside me like a volcano that was about to erupt. I slid to my knees at the foot of the bed as the tears poured down my cheeks and my body shook in uncontrollable sobs.

The softness of the plush carpet did not comfort me at all, nor did the fancy wallpaper, the lovely furniture, the in-ground heated pool nor the profitable business my husband and I owned. These material things enabled me to be comfortable, but they did not COMFORT me. Inside my heart there was no happy face at all; years of wounds had been accumulating until my heart could contain no more.

Thirteen years is a long, long, time to live in an unhappy marriage. As each day passed, fear managed to get a tighter grip on me in many different ways. If someone turned around in our driveway I knew when my husband got home he would ask me whose tracks were in the driveway, who had come, and continue to harass me. He even came home at times on his coffee break to check up on what I was doing. He was extremely jealous and would not trust anyone, least of all me.

Eleven years after we were married I discovered that a woman he dated before meeting me, left him for an older man. He never got over it.

That was like a light bulb coming on and I told him I felt like I paid for eleven years for what she did because of his jealousy! I served notice that I would not give in to it ever again.

This revelation caused bitterness between my husband and I that certainly was not healthy. Two wrongs don't make a right. Jealousy smothers and kills love. Insecurity is at the root and beneath that usually is fear. I did not know that then, so I was bitter.

Now we were separated, but that was not the reason for the tears. They were shed for my son. I had not seen him for over two months and it seemed like years. The straw that broke the camel's back was the fact that today was his birthday.

My thoughts returned to the day of his birth. He was 8 lb. 8 oz. and absolutely perfect as far as I was concerned. We brought him home from the hospital on Father's Day, appropriately enough. When I walked out of the hospital with him in my arms it was the proudest and happiest moment of my life. My heart pounded so hard with excitement I thought it would burst!

Almost twelve years had passed and I wondered where the time went. I recalled his first Christmas; first tooth, first steps, first words, first injury, first tears, first black eye after falling onto an open oven door, first birthday party, first haircut, first ride on a toboggan and snowmobile, first bicycle, first day at school, first report card, first ride on a tractor, first time he looked at a cow "eyeball to eyeball", first time he used a hammer and saw, first time he ventured out to sell Halloween candy, first time he went fishing and fell into the creek.

The first time he and I went on a Ferris Wheel and when it stopped with us at the top he got brave and started rocking the seat...much to my horror, first time on skates, first big test at school, first boat ride, first school bus ride, first time pushing a wheelbarrow, first time helping to bake.....and eating the icing out of the bowl, first card game, first time at Sunday school, first time using the lawnmower, first time cleaning the aquarium, first time staying overnight with his best friend, first time purchasing some fish for the aquarium, first trip to the library, and the doctor, and the dentist, first Mother's day card he made me, first Christmas gift he wrapped himself, first time he asked me about the "birds and the bees", first time he sat at the kitchen table doing homework, first time we went for a walk just to go for a walk...........all day long a list of his "firsts" would pass through my mind.

Once he called me and when I looked out the kitchen window I saw my five-year old boy wearing rubber boots on a sunny day, trying to walk through a field of hay that was higher than he was and he carried high over his shoulder a six-foot long pole with a large fish net on the other end of it and he said, **"I'M CATCHING BUTTERFLIES!!"** (even a bird could have escaped through the holes in the fish net.)

One particular disciplinary measure I clearly recalled was when he was around five years old, and swore at me for the first time....and LAST time! I packed a little suitcase and grabbed him by the arm as I ushered him out the back door, handed him the suitcase and said, "If you think you are going to swear you've got another think coming. You are not going to talk like that around here, ever, so just take your suitcase and go and when you get hungry, don't come back here, and when you get cold, don't come back here. You can't stay here if you are going to talk like that!" Then I shut the door. (At this point I was actually surprised at my own action because this happened so quickly I didn't have time to really think about it, I just did it.) He (needless to say) was in tears and I'm sure was as surprised at what had happened as I was. Nevertheless, he learned a lesson and he never forgot it because he never once swore at me again. (In hindsight, I'd suggest a less severe disciplinary measure, although it did work. I did it so I am sharing the truth. I've not met one parent that doesn't wish they did something different in the raising of their children.)

His first spanking hurt me much more than him, I'm sure. I recalled the surprised look on his face when he received his first phone call, and also recalled his first swim, first baseball mitt, first time viewing new photographs together, first hockey game and first trip via an airplane.

One year we did things a little differently with a particular Christmas gift for him. We had purchased a minibike for him and were determined to keep it a surprise. Since we didn't want to risk hiding it at home we made arrangements to leave it at our next-door neighbors. We told them the four of us would arrive sometime Christmas morning to pick up the bike.

The two single sisters who lived there, were as excited as we were when Christmas morning arrived. They loved our children too and were always good to them. With much excitement, we arrived and tried to leave the snow outside. They told my son there was something in the hall and it didn't take him long to find it! It was a very joyous moment for everyone.

The first time he saw his new baby sister (8 lb. 12 oz.) he looked down at her in the hospital nursery and said, (**"She's not little, she's big!"**) then he looked at me standing in the doorway of my hospital room and said, **"Mommy, you lost your tummy!"**

He used to pull weeds AND plants in the garden, first time using clippers on the shrubs, first time using a paint brush, first time playing bumper with Grandpop and Grammie (bumper is a game my dad taught us using a board he spent hours making, as well as using cards and marbles), first time climbing a tree, first time raking leaves in a neat pile then jumping in them, first time dancing with his sister and I, first time using a tape recorder (he was a great news broadcaster/reporter and sang duets with his sister), first time making his own bed, first camera, first time on skis, first time milking a cow, first time he picked fresh flowers from a field - including a dandelion and gave them to me, first time he had to eat liver, first time he made popcorn, first egg he cracked, first dog we had for more than a few months (Laddie).

First ride in a big gravel truck and on a bulldozer, first pumpkin he carved, and the second, and the third, with neighbor kids, first wad of gum he stuck on the headboard of his bed, first time in the hospital was to have his tonsils removed when he was not yet two, and when his bed became damp... he crawled into the empty bed next to it! (smart boy), first time he set the table and reversed the silverware but the rest was perfect, first thing he did when returning from school was give me a hug and kiss, first thing he did as soon as dinner was over was say "thanks for the supper" and give me a kiss, first thing after preparing for bed was saying his prayers, and on and on and on. **The memories are endless and PRICELESS!!!**

There are thousands of FIRSTS I recalled over the years until I reached the present time. Then, the firsts became the lasts, because it had been over two months since I had seen him.

I began to remember the last time he hugged me and told me he loved me the last time he talked to me on the phone, and then I could not allow myself to remember any more because the hurt was too much to bear. Two months seemed a lifetime and I could not take any more of this hurt. I sat on the floor next to my bed and allowed the tears to pour down my cheeks like a river as the hurt spilled from full to overflowing. My cup runneth over with hurt. When the racking sobs subsided, I wiped my face with a towel and reached out to move a slipper out of the way. I noticed a little piece of black paper resting on the heel and brushed it with my hand but it did not move. I picked up the gold slipper and got the biggest shock!

There was a piece of black thick paper stuck firmly to the heel and there were perfectly formed letters printed on this paper in white. It looked like chalk but it wasn't and it was not ink. I'll never know for sure what it was until I meet my Maker.

The letters formed the words **"Bride of the Lord"**. The words were enclosed in a shape like a figure eight except the center did not join together. Two words were at the top and two words at the bottom of this little piece of paper, and in the center was the outline in white of one perfect maple leaf.

> *I thought I was going to faint, then I felt something go right through my body that made me draw even closer to the floor because I KNEW this was the power of GOD! I had the fear of the Lord for the first time in my life and I felt so small and insignificant that I could not get down low enough to show the respect I knew He deserved. He is so HOLY!*

Something happened, he touched me and filled me with his love. He turned my mourning into joy, my mouth gave praise to the Lord. I looked at the slipper again and had a visitor called "the devil" right there with me.

He said, "That's not from God, someone put it there, someone came in the house and stuck that on the slipper when you weren't looking. Someone has been in your bedroom. There is someone you can't trust. Who is it?" I thought for a minute and remembered vacuuming two days before and moving the slippers at that time and knew the sticker was not there then. I backtracked in time and knew no one had been at my home for eleven days so I tossed aside what I thought were my thought......actually they were the devil's effort to deceive.

The power of God is something you cannot deny. When it comes upon you, you will KNOW it, and you will KNOW it is the power of GOD, not anyone or anything else!

I stood up and joy was bubbling inside my veins. I couldn't stand still. I looked at the slipper in my hand and the word Bride was all I could see for the moment. I opened my closet door and took out my wedding dress I had worn thirteen years previously. I KNEW I never felt this good when I put it on then, because I had never felt so good in my life!

The dress looked so inviting and even though it hadn't been worn for thirteen years it fit perfectly.

Praise God.   I put the gold slippers on quickly, then pinned a nametag on my dress.   I felt urged to take this pin out of my jewelry box and wear it. It showed the skip name I had used for ten years when I was operating a Citizens Band radio.   The name is "Rainbow".   Now things were complete, and my dancing feet left the bedroom.

Inside my body I felt like a pop bottle someone had been shaking while the cap was still on tightly. I knew my feet were there but I couldn't even feel them. I was so high.   The rivers of love and joy poured through my inner being.   Into the living-room I ran, yards and yards of material in my long gown flowing as I danced circles around the coffee table, my face absolutely glowing.

There could never have been a smile bigger than the one I wore.   Never in my life had I felt this good and I knew it was nothing I had done, but GOD who caused this love to overflow and replace the hurt that was there previously. I did not know anyone could be so alive, so happy, so fired up.

It kept increasing and I really thought I would explode!

All this dancing and excitement resulted in my getting quite warm so I opened the front door, then wondered about the neighbors across the road. There was no car in my driveway, so they would know I was home alone and if they saw me fly by the big living-room window (the drapes were open) wearing a wedding gown they might phone the police, thinking I was off my rocker for sure. (If this was what being off your rocker was like then I was ALL FOR IT!!!) Of course, that was the sly devil trying to stop all my happiness by making me afraid of what others would do or say.

God was there and he was in control and though my relationship with him was very new, I was certain in my heart that I would not have company, or be disturbed at all as I danced about in my wedding gown. The entire evening was for God and I and no one else.

I danced and skipped through every room of the house, my hands swishing the big skirt from one side to the other. If my head was ever above the clouds and my feet on the ground (barely) it was that evening! I did not have a vision of the Lord, but I could see him in my mind's eye and he was smiling from ear to ear!

As I practically floated from one room to another material things looked so different. I now saw through God's eyes and realized a new beauty in many things as his love flowed. One flower was transformed from pretty or lovely to exquisite as each petal had a purpose and came alive. Alone, yet so compete and this was how I felt!

Over to the electric organ I went. As I sat on the bench my flowing gown formed a cover around the bench and one gold slipper aimed for the foot pedal. The only hymn I ever learned to play is what I began to play then: **"Jesus Loves Me"**!

How beautiful to see part of God's plan for me unfold. When I was six or seven years of age I took piano lessons from my Aunt. Little did we realize how important a part this particular lesson would play many years later. Praise God. I played Jesus Loves Me again and again. The more I played it, the louder I played it, and the louder I played it the louder I sang, and the louder I sang the more God's love flowed through every pore.

This happened on June 16, 1976, my son's twelfth birthday, and though I knew it was God working in my life I did not have the spiritual understanding and guidance that is so necessary to effectively serve God. Twenty-eight long months passed before I found out what really happened to me: I had been baptized in love by God's almighty hand and God's power!

The Gold Slipper

Tears poured down my cheeks
As my body shook in uncontrollable sobs
I slid to my knees at the foot of the bed
The plush carpet did not impress me at all

Nor did the fancy wallpaper
The beautiful furniture
The in-ground pool
Or the profitable business my husband owned

The reality of it all
Was inside my heart
There were no happy faces at all
Years of wounds did my heart recall

Thirteen years in an unhappy marriage
Is a long, long, time
It is incredible what fear can do to a person
The fear kept me in bondage for all those years

Now we were separated
But that was not the reason for the tears
They were shed for my son, I had not seen
A few months seemed like years

As the tears subsided
My arm reached for a gold slipper near me
I tried to brush off a piece of black paper
It was resting on the heel

When it did not move I picked up the slipper
And got the shock of my life
The black marker was sealed to the heel
With this written on it
"Bride of the Lord."

The letters were perfectly shaped
And written in white
So tiny I couldn't imagine how it was done
And in the center in white was a perfect maple leaf

I literally collapsed to the floor
In my heart, I knew God did this
Only He could show me so beautifully
That He was aware of my trials and did care
Satan was right there too, you can be sure

Trying to put doubt in my mind
as to who put this there

No one had been at my home for eleven days
And the slipper was not marked
just a few days earlier
I felt certain I would have noticed when I cleaned
So satan didn't get far with me
I was so grateful to God for showing me this
And touched to the depths of my soul

I washed the tears away
And opened the door of the closet
My wedding dress never looked so inviting
I put it on, and the gold slippers as well

The Lord spoke to me about a pin I owned
I quickly put it on, **'RAINBOW'** is what it said
It was my skip name on Citizens
Band radio for ten years
I wasn't sure the connection then
but obeyed God's request

I literally ran into the living room
Yards of material in my long gown flowing
As I danced circles around the coffee table

My face absolutely glowing

There couldn't have ever been a smile
Bigger than the one I wore that night
I had never felt so good in my entire life
And it was ONLY GOD who made it right

I didn't know anyone could be so happy
I actually thought I would explode
I opened the front door, it was so warm
Then wondered about the neighbors across the road

They would know from the driveway
I was home alone
And if they saw me fly by the win-
dow in a wedding gown
I'm sure the police, they would phone

ONLY for a second did the thought concern me
Because somehow, in my heart I just knew
I would not have company, or be disturbed
This entire evening was for God
and I and only us two

I danced all through the house
Then over to the electric organ

Sat down and started to play
The only hymn I ever did learn

Jesus Loves Me!
How very appropriate it seemed
Each time I played it louder
And absolutely beamed

The joy flowed through my every pore
It is something I'll not forget as long as I live
Only God could make a human feel like this
And to him I want to give

That happened over three years ago
Praise God because now I understand
I believe I was baptized in love
By God's almighty hand!

CHAPTER 7

Angel Wings

IT WAS A very hot summer day and I decided to go for a short drive in the country. Just as I started down the road I felt something in my back. I leaned forward on the steering wheel, waiting for this thing whatever it was, to fall. It didn't.

I rested back but something was still preventing me from resting against the seat. When I tried to press my back into the seat, I couldn't, it actually hurt. Yet, I couldn't SEE anything!

It felt like I had actually grown WINGS! At first, I was afraid to look in the rear-view mirror in case I saw a big wing extended up there above my shoulder. What a sensation! It would NOT go away, yet I could not SEE anything. I managed to summon up enough courage to look in the mirror. I continued to drive but this was very aggravating. In each shoulder blade I actually felt a nodule extend and when I leaned back too far it hurt.

I drove for about ten miles and the presence of God was so strong in the car I did not know what to expect. If I turned and actually saw Jesus in the flesh sitting on the seat next to me it would not have surprised me. It truly would not have because so much had been happening that I knew was God's doing and no one else's, that I thought He must be preparing me for something very special though WHAT I did not know.

The poem "Angel Wings" was not actually written until after I became a born-again Christian and began to grow spiritually by attending a church teaching the full gospel. A remark made by the Pastor (and shared in the following poem.) spurred me to write the poem in order to share yet another of the glorious ways in which God ministers to us. *He has a good sense of humor, to say the least.* (FYI: I don't care if I get criticized about this because to me it was a special touch from God, so special I chose to share because His ways are… higher.)

Angel Wings

I was driving down a country road
On a hot summer day
When I felt something
Getting in the way

It wasn't an object on the road
It was something on my back
I leaned forward and shrugged my shoulders
But the answer I did lack

A nodule was on each shoulder blade
Preventing me from resting against the seat
When I did, it hurt
I thought, "It must be the seat."

I continued to drive
But this was very aggravating
It felt like I had actually grown wings

I didn't dare look in the rear-
view mirror, I kept waiting

This sensation lasted throughout my ten-mile drive
I sensed the presence of God so strong
And marveled at the wonderful ways
In which he encourages us along

A few years had passed
And I hadn't written of the experience
Until our Pastor's sermon one Sunday
This poem was written hence

He made a remark about each of us
Not having any trouble
Tucking our wings under our coat
To get to church

I wanted to say "I DID!"
But bit my tongue
Now I feel it is time to share the different ways
God ministers, to everyone!

CHAPTER 8

The High Sign

How MANY PEOPLE can and will say they actually **SAW a miracle**? I can and I give God the glory for what He did for my family.

My daughter was eight years old and we visited my mother on her birthday. When we arrived, my father was not home. As mom and I continued visiting, my daughter had gone outside to play in the sand. She had gone too close to the road so I stepped outside and spoke to her. Just then I heard an airplane overhead and as I looked skyward, I heard my daughter say, **"Mommy, what is the plane saying? It's a letter, LOOK!"** Then she spoke aloud two words, **"Help Love"** then she spelled letter by letter what her eyes saw: **"G R A M M I E ."**

I saw it all and never took my eyes off the sky and the plane, but I never said a word. At first, I thought I was seeing things until her voice I heard. Her lips confirmed what I saw. Also, she was eight years and three months and could not read the word Grammie, or spell it, but she spoke each letter aloud after reading it in the sky.

The letters were formed in the jet stream. Never have I seen this happen before or since.

My mother heard us call her to see but by the time she arrived on the porch, the letters were blurred. Her eyes filled with tears when we told her what we saw.

Suddenly, the impact of these words came. I knew it had nothing to do with mom's birthday. It was a fact that we had just discovered my father had cancer less than a month before. Consequently, my concern for him was very great, especially since at that point my husband and son were gone from the family scene.

For mom and dad not to be able to see their grandson this was a real heartbreak to both of them. Their hair turned gray so fast it was incredible. Also, their concern and worry for me because of a broken marriage was taking its toll.

Now, I saw what God wanted me to see. All my attention was going to my father whom I loved so much; yet my mother needed more strength than ever before. If she was not comforted and encouraged and strengthened it would be her I would be grieving for.

How wonderful it is to serve a God who cares so much he did this to prove his deep concern for each of us. He will never leave us, nor forsake us! **Hebrews 13:5 "Let your conversation be without covetousness; and be content with such things as ye have; for he hath said, I will never leave thee, nor forsake thee."**

The High Sign

I saw a miracle
On my mother's birthday, June 17
My daughter saw it too
We want to share it with you

My mother and I were inside visiting
While my daughter played in the sand
I became concerned of her nearness to the road
So went out to guide her hand

As we walked to the front lawn
We heard an airplane overhead
We both looked skyward
And this is what my daughter said

"Mommy, what is the plane saying?
It's writing a letter, look!"
"Help love GRAMMIE."

I saw all of this
But never said a word
I thought I was seeing things
Until her voice I heard

She had seen it too and if her lips confirmed
What I saw
She couldn't identify the last word
But spelled it all

She was just eight years old
And to this day remembers
The letters were formed in the jet stream
Never have I seen this happen again...yet

I was stunned for so long
I was slow in calling my mom
When she arrived outside
The words were too blurred

She shed tears
When we shared what we saw
This revelation from God
Had me in awe

I felt I knew
The message God was trying to convey
It had nothing to do
With Mom's birthday

The fact is that we had just discovered
My father had cancer.
My concern was very great for him
But should also have been for HER!

I was only too aware
Of the heartache there had already been
Because of my broken marriage
And her grandson she had not seen

With the additional concern for my dad
Mom needed more strength than ever before
If she wasn't comforted,
Strengthened and encouraged
It could easily be more than she could endure

This proved to me
In such a simple but beautiful way
God's concern for each of us
Every single day

CHAPTER 9

Summary of Miracles

THE LAST THREE poems "The Gold Slipper, Angel wings, and The High Sign", all tell how God has ministered to me. More important than the miracles is what I have come to realize since I have grown spiritually.

I am not proud to point out that the incident with the Gold Slipper did not result in my rushing to church. **I knew God did this, no doubt in my mind, but I also thought I was a Christian and that this was why God gave me this miracle.**

Talk about self-righteous! I didn't even attend church, and it is obvious I did not have the fear of the Lord. If only we could realize and understand how much the Lord loves us. Even though I was not serving or acknowledging Him, He did all these things for me because He loves me so much, and He is no respecter of persons. He loves everyone.

I admit I spent a lot of time thinking about the gold slipper, and so many times I have regretted wearing it because the letters and maple leaf wore off from wear. *If there ever was a Cinderella in real life it was me when these slippers, I wore! At least that is how I felt.*

I even phoned an elderly lady one day and during our conversation I said that I am a Bride of the Lord. She asked me how I knew. I then shared what happened to my slipper and she did not know what to say. She may still be scratching her head about it.

As for the Angel Wings, it was a sensation I will never forget. I am grateful to God for performing this miracle in my life, in yet another attempt to draw me closer to him.

The High Sign definitely touched my heart; that God was so good to warn me about my mother's health, and instilled a certain amount of fear of the Lord. *Nevertheless, I still didn't turn to Him in prayer and thanksgiving on any kind of a regular basis.*

Now that I attend church regularly, read the Bible daily, listen to tapes of Christian teaching, and Christian music; I have become aware of what I am sure are only a few of my shortcomings.

I realize all the miracles God has shown me, the many ways in which He tried to impress upon me how much he desired to have me lean on him, and open my heart. Though I was as a filthy rag, as far as my righteousness was concerned, He still loved me and nudged me ever so gently to open my eyes and ears to His wondrous ways.

I asked myself, and I ask you: **How many friends do we have that would give us as much attention as God does even though we did not respond to their attention? Chances are, most human beings would turn to someone else with their attention.**

I rejected the way into fellowship with God through his son, Jesus Christ. How many times has God shown you miracles, nudged you in certain areas, spoke to you, all to no avail because you were too self-centered or too preoccupied with things of the world to acknowledge him? Think about it. Search your heart.

It is bad enough to hurt a husband, wife, parent or child, but to grieve the Holy Spirit is terrible. It is yourself you hurt more than anyone else. It is the devil; satan, who does not want you to acknowledge the miracles God has given you, nor does he want you to give God the glory.

I'm a fool for Jesus. Whose fool, are you?

Summary of Miracles

Just because I received miracles
Did not result in me
Getting into right relationship with God
One may wonder how this could be

My heart was touched many times
Yet my understanding of spiritual things
Was strictly head knowledge
Not heart knowledge revealed by the Holy Spirit

My search for peace continued
God continued too
He lovingly encouraged me to open my heart
But leaning on Him I didn't know HOW to do

He never gave up on me
I know human beings would
Because there were a lot that did
Not God though, and if he wanted to he could

God hasn't given up on you either
How many miracles has He shown or give you
We hurt ourselves by rejecting Him
Yet often, this is what we do

I'm so thankful God is patient
He knocked on the door of my heart for years
I doubt that any human being would knock that long
Knowing God's love and patience
Brought forth many tears

He protected me many times
Yet from him, I walked away
Such love only God can give
And with God, I'll stay

His Son, I now know personally
He is my best Friend too
I'm a fool for Jesus
Whose fool, are you?

CHAPTER 10

Emptiness

THERE IS SO much hustle and bustle as people hurry about to do their Christmas shopping. Traffic jams are not uncommon and frayed nerves are under the tension filled faces as people wonder how the extra expenses will be paid.

It is the saddest time of the year for those who are alone. Since I had not seen my son for months and it was very doubtful I would see him for Christmas, the last thing on my mind was a desire to buy Christmas cards and a tree.

There was no hustle, no bustle for me. I did not want to admit I missed the excitement and planning even though there always seemed to be a last-minute rush in previous years. I did buy cards and a tree, but my thoughts were not about Christ's birthday; my thoughts were on me. Poor, poor, little sad me. Time could not pass quickly enough for me.

I was so full of self-pity, so depressed, so broke, so worried about finances, I could not see anything but negative, negative, negative. There was no desire to bake, no desire to do anything but wait for time to pass because I thought time was the only answer at that point. I did pray once in a while but since things looked so glum my prayer attitude left a lot to be desired. If you can't pray believing don't expect to be receiving!

There weren't many records but I played them again and again. Wasted time fantasizing about how I wanted things to be, rather than facing reality. Fantasizing enabled me to escape reality momentarily and it was a cheap way of relieving pain. Alcohol and pills cost money, but fantasy was free. Well, not really because each thought lead to another and it was denial of reality.

The extent of my goal setting that next year was that custody of my son would be finalized in court and my divorce would be through. I told myself I would have a good job and a special friend to talk to. I was so sure this slave driven wife would be a liberated woman when the red tape was through and a whole new life would be waiting for me. *But for now, I was very empty. No spark or glow.*

Emptiness

It's that time of year again.
Hustle, bustle, traffic jams, nerves frayed
Faces filled with tension and worry
Wondering how the extra expenses will be paid
It is the saddest time for those who are alone
No need to buy cards or a tree
No hustle, bustle, extra expense
Alone with their problems, like me
Oh, I bought cards
And I've got a tree
But the spirit's not there
Because it's just me
No desire to bake
Cookies and squares
No Christmas pudding
Just lots of prayers
I play a love song
And fantasize a while
Dreaming helps ease the pain

And prepare me for a smile
I pull my chin way up high
Raise my eyes to the sky
Set some goals for '77
And pray to heaven
Next year custody will be decided
My divorce will be through
I'll have a good job
And a special friend to talk to

CHAPTER 11

Anticipation

IT HAS BEEN over a year since I saw my precious son. The same question keeps popping up in my mind, when will my daughter and I see him again? Sometimes the time is not too long, but other times the burden is so heavy I can hardly bear it. I think of all the questions he used to ask and now there are no more questions. I think of how much a child grows in just one year and wonder how tall he is, how much he weighs, if he still wears his favorite baseball cap, etc.

Then I wonder how he is doing in school, if he likes his teacher and peers. I miss all the things he used to share with me when he came home from school each day. I won't allow myself to think about all the changes he is going through that I am no longer a part of because it hurts too much.

There has been much for him to endure as with every-one involved but I know one thing for sure. God has blessed us for our endurance, and most important of all: I am a born again Christian and will share the joy. I will write a lot of poems so he will know how I feel. I will also write a book that will show my love for him and it will explain a lot of things to him. The truth will be in the book and the truth will make his head reel. There are two sides to every story and this is my way of showing the truth.

(I knew of the term "born-again" but at this point in my life I had no knowledge of what this really meant; and the necessity of reading the Bible, attending church services, and fellowshipping with fruit bearing Christians. I was reaching out to God, but did not know anything about a personal relationship with Jesus Christ!)

Anticipation

When will we see him again
Where will we meet
It's been over a year
Since we held each other
Cheek to cheek
Some days it gets really, really hard
No son to love and give advice to
But soon these hard times
We won't have to endure
Because the Lord has blessed us
For our endurance…
Of that
I am sure
There is one plus
For the pain we went through
I am a born again Christian
And will share the joy
With you
I'll write lots of poems

So you'll know how I feel
I'll also write a book
That will make your head reel!

CHAPTER 12

My Daddy

MY DADDY HAS always been and still is a man I have respected all my life. He is the kind of man everyone likes and was a great blessing to me particularly during the first eighteen months after my marriage broke up. He was like the yeast in the bread because he kept things working.

He and mom took my daughter and I out to dinner periodically. Either that, or a visit to the store for soft ice cream in the summer. When people see him smile, they smile in return. He is the reason for the happy faces on those he meets.

My home was in a rural area and I did not own a car. My father had two cars and gave me one to use. He loaned me money so I could meet the mortgage payments on the house which I had listed for sale. He repaired the lawnmower and vacuumed the pool. Also helped winterize it and look after the heater and filtering system. He also repaired the car. There was never a refusal to help. ***He always was there when I needed him.***

He is a husband, father, grandpop, friend, and I thank him for all the times he took time to help me in my time of need. I love him so much and I am praying for his salvation.

Daddy

He is a man that is FRANK, (Pardon the pun.)
Generous, honest and sincere
Gentle, kind, loyal
It's great when he's here

He is so handsome
With his masculine physique
His dark brown eyes
And a smile in his cheek

He is always pleasant
Easygoing and fun
Friendly to all
Foe to none

He takes me to dinner
He's always buying treats
He's the reason for the happy faces
On everyone he meets

He loaned me his car
He loaned me some money
He never complained
He's a real honey

He fixed the lawnmower
He vacuumed the pool
He repaired the car
He's no fool!

He's a husband
He's a father
He's a grandpop
He's a friend
He's my dad
I love him!

THE END
☺

CHAPTER 13

Family

MY DAUGHTER AND I realized something very important this Christmas. As time was spent with relatives nearly five hundred miles from our home, and more relatives continued to cross our path as we visited from house to house, we realized how proud we were to be part of this family. With Aunts, Grandpas, Grammies, cousins, twins, the names are not important, what is important is the fact that they were ladies and gentlemen and respected by many.

They are givers, not takers. They knew I was separated from my husband and son, yet they made me feel so welcome and at home. They knew I ached and hurt inside, yet there was not much they could do, as far as solving these problems. But, they realized they could help simply by loving me and showing compassion. This is what they did and it was a great healing balm for me.

The love and compassion they showed changed my way of thinking considerably. Instead of arriving with an attitude of, "Well, here we are, like half a team, incomplete and I suppose everyone will want to hear all the details about what happened...why the marriage breakdown?" My attitude changed when they received me in the way in which they did.

I had been thinking that "family" meant two, because that was the sum of my daughter and I. Consequently, when I was at the dinner table Christmas day and saw so many relatives looking back at me, I realized my family consisted of a lot more than two. My daughter and I are not just one or two; we are a tiny part of quite a few.

The fact that many of us live miles apart, somehow didn't matter anymore, because I now realized we were like two members of a baseball team. Together, we could still play ball, or with the rest of the family we could play ball too, only on a larger scale. We could have more members on our team when we were all together, but the point is: either way we continue playing ball. The family does not cease to function; it continues to be productive, as long as the members continue to love each other.

The Christmas gift of love and continued acceptance of she and I to the family, was the greatest gift I could have received. True love heals and removes all barriers. The pictures will remind us of all the fun, and the memories we will cherish for years to come.

Family

We are not one
Nor are we two
We are a tiny part
Of quite a few
With Aunts and Grandpas
Cousins and twins
We are proud to be
In the family we're in
Graham, Winslow
Jones and Wood
Being part of such a family
Sure makes one feel good
They are ladies, they are gentlemen
They are respected by many
They're givers, not takers
And enemies, they don't have any
This Christmas has been special
For my daughter and me
Made special by members

Final Request

Of our family
The memories we'll cherish
For years to come
The pictures will remind us
Of all the fun

121

CHAPTER 14

Joy

ONE DAY I looked at my daughter and saw her in a way I had never seen her before. Instead of seeing my problems regardless of which way I turned, I saw a little girl that was so full of joy and love that I couldn't help being affected by her in a very positive way.

I think I wrote this poem when she was about eight or nine years old. This poem has a very special place in my heart because it was a turning point for me. A point when I began to stop looking at my problems and be optimistic about things when I saw how much I had right in front of me for which to be thankful. When we continue to look at our problems instead of the answers we continue to remain depressed and in a slump. The day I realized the following, is the day I got out of a slump.

I took time to really look at my little girl's face when she said, **"I love you, mommy."** *I listened to the tone of her voice and allowed the love to be received as she reached out to me.*

The look on her face as she sampled her first batch of cookies was one of such urgency. It was so important to her that the cookies be good. As she bit into the cookie one might have thought she was biting a grenade because of the tortured look on her face. Then the expression turned to a crummy smile, (pardon the pun) as here eyes lit up in delight. **Success!!**

Every once in a while, I awoke in the morning to sounds coming from the kitchen. Soon, I heard the pitter patter of footsteps as they approached my bedroom door. In walked my daughter carrying a big tray with breakfast. She did things in style too. Not just a coffee mug and a piece of toast. She had cereal, toast, jam, teacup and saucer and a pot of tea, cream and sugar, and to top it all a vase with a flower and next to it, a lit candle. It was all she could do to carry it all. *I don't know who was shining more brightly, her or the candle.*

The satisfaction she got out of doing this herself and the excitement she felt by surprising me would touch anyone's heart. As the months passed, she became more experienced (Not daily, this was an occasional treat.) and at one point brought tea first with a menu consisting of juice, tea, coffee, cereal, toast, French toast, eggs or pancakes. Mind you, there were other changes too by this time. **Now she was checking the empty tray for a tip!** ☺

Joy is when she would hop off the school bus and literally run to the door. She never dragged her feet or walked slowly. There was a purpose in what she did and she ran to the door anxious to be home with mommy.

Some children return home from school to a locked door. Their mother working, they search for their key and step into a room with no one there to greet them with a hug, kiss, smile. They feel only empty and alone. Other children return home to find mommy so engrossed in watching soap operas on television she can only tell the child to shut up. They receive rejection the instant they return home.

Still other children return home to the sitter whose language leaves much to be desired. Sometimes a mature reliable sitter is there and this warmth is certainly needed. Someone with an understanding heart is needed to comfort children who have experienced how cruel their playmates can be.

The child needs the comfort, right then, while the wound is open and fresh, not after it has had time to fester and become infected with bitterness and hatred. Children need to communicate too. If there is no loving vessel for them to open up to, deep scarring can result as they carry the hurts and pains of growing up inside them, sometimes for many years until the hurts build up and the person becomes a walking volcano about to erupt.

If only more parents would be parents instead of idolizing the dollar and placing more importance on owning a second television or second car, there would be fewer juvenile delinquents. The parents and the child are robbed of the time they need together to communicate and strengthen family ties, and time cannot be stockpiled. It is the only thing we all have an equal measure of; twenty-four hours in each day.

Joy is when I hear my daughter giggle as we play together. There is something about a child's laughter that rings through to your soul. You can't help being positively affected by it. Even a child who speaks a language you do not understand can touch your heart with his/her laughter.

Some of the greatest times we have had together have been when I humbled myself and became childlike too. Crawling around on one's knees on all fours is not silly to do. When you bring yourself to a child's level you can relate to them like never before.

After a time of tickling and playing together, my daughter and I sat side by side and enjoyed some very personal and intimate conversations. She and I were both more relaxed and ready to open our hearts to each other as the door to communicate was open. Each time this happened our trust in each other grew as did our love as we shared as only a mother and daughter can. I looked forward to having her home all day on Saturday.

Seeing a curly haired child hop in and out the door what seemed like thousands of times a day, did something to me. Each entrance was like a shot of adrenalin as I looked at her sweet joyous face and wondered what was on her mind next. I never knew what was going to come out of her mouth, but then I guess we never know what is going to come out of anyone's mouth.

I recall one day when she wore a new pair of blue jeans. She was so excited and happy over them that I wondered if I would be able to get them off her at bedtime. They fit perfectly and she looked so cute as she wiggled about in them.

Joy is when she wore a little dress I had made for her (the first) that was the same material and style as mine. The idolism in her eyes and the closeness we felt was touching. Joy is when we would open our hands; lay them on the table side by side as we compared the length of our half-bitten fingernails. Each insisting her nails were longer. I think I've bit mine ever since I grew teeth, and have struggled for years to be free of this habit until the last few months. So far, so good and she is improving too.

Joy is when she runs to the mailbox and there is a letter for her. ***If more people only knew how much a letter can mean to others, many more letters would be written.***

Many times, she would go for a walk in the back field and return home with a bouquet of wild flowers in her hands. **"Here Mommy, they're for you."** Daisies, buttercups, a few weeds as well, pretty, but not nearly as pretty as her face when she gave so freely. She did this so many times even though dandelion stains on here hands had to be scrubbed off later.

So many times, she would come home from the store with a little gift for me. Anything from a package of gum to a chocolate bar, depending on the amount of money she had. Recently, she bought me a wire bound notebook and a new pen with her babysitting money. She is twelve now. She called it an early birth-day present, though my birthday is a month away. She gives with no strings attached and I think this is beautiful. After all, God loveth a cheerful giver, **2 Corinthians 9:7 "Every man according as he purpos-eth in his heart, so let him give; not grudgingly, or of necessity: for God loveth a cheerful giver,"**

Joy is when she is so thoughtful concerning others. She knows what it is to be deeply hurt as a child, after being separated from her father and her brother, so is deeply conscious of the feelings of others. She gives to friends without being told and has many friends because she has learned to first, reach out and be friendly to others. She doesn't stand around and wait for others to come to her, she extends herself. You reap what you sow.

For a while I was selling household cleaners and she sold some at school to the teachers. She did not want the commission she earned. Her joy was in doing the selling.

Joy is when she sings and sings and sings, like a bird that is rejoicing. She has a lovely voice and was always singing a new song she learned in the school choir.

Joy is when she looked at the clock and told the time correctly. When she was first learning to tell time, she would be so elated when she did it correctly.

Joy is when the final day of school arrives and she brings her report card home with a smile on her face. A smile because she passed!

Joy is being in another room and hearing her laughter echo through the house as she watches cartoons. She has the heartiest giggle and many are affected in a joyous way by it.

Joy is when she says her prayers every night, without fail. Never is she hesitant or too tired, she is faithful, even though at this time in our lives we did not know Jesus in a personal way. Her prayer was a memorized prayer that my brother and I repeated night after night when we were kids. I shared this prayer earlier, "Now I lay me, down to sleep......"

Joy is having a daughter that loves you and is the fulfillment of your childhood dreams as to what a daughter is: even more than what you thought a daughter could be. *Joy is having the daughter I have; love me as much as I love her!*

Joy

Joy is when she says
I love you Mommy
Joy is the smile on her face
As she samples her first batch of cookies
Joy is when she brings me breakfast in bed
Including a candle
Joy is when she hops off the school bus
And runs to the door
Joy is when she giggles
As we have a play
Joy is when she is with me
ALL day
Joy is when she looks so cute
In her new blue jeans
Joy is when she dresses like mommy
Idolism in her eyes
Joy is when we compare the length
Of our half-bitten nails
Joy is when a letter is for her

In the mail
Joy is when she brings me flowers
After a walk in the fields
Joy is when she spends her allowance on me
Sharing
Joy is when she is so thoughtful
And gives to others without being told
Joy is when she sells Amway
Without a commission
Joy is when she sings
Like a bird
Joy is when she tells time
And it is right
Joy is when she brings her report card home
With a smile on her face
Joy is the sound of her laughter
When she watches cartoons
Joy is when she says her prayers every night
Without fail
Joy is having a daughter
Just like your dreams!

CHAPTER 15

Longings

THERE ARE TIMES my chesterfield becomes very long especially when I am lonely. Adjusting to living alone, as opposed to living with a husband is not an adjustment that happens in a day or two. Loneliness is a disease responsible for killing many people. They die a slow agonizing death. I found one way to overcome the loneliness and the physical desires my flesh cried out for.

There were times I would lie on the chesterfield to relax and as I looked down at my feet, the chesterfield seemed so big, so empty, so long. It seemed twenty feet long and I was not capable of filling it. An overwhelming urge to cry filled my body. Being alone is so terrible. I crossed my arms in front of me in an effort to hug myself, to comfort myself. My eyes filled with tears as I looked up at the blank ceiling. It seemed so far away from me too. I longed to gaze up and see a man's eyes looking back into mine, returning my longing. I needed a man's arms around me, not my own. I needed his warmth, not the warmth of a blanket, his voice in my ear is what I wanted to hear, not the voice on a record.

As I lay there, longing for a man tears began to well up in my eyes until they overflowed and ran down the side of my face into my ear. My longings for a man were overcome as soon as the tears entered my ears because off to the bathroom I ran. My mascara ran all over my face. Suddenly I didn't have time for self-pity any more. I had no time to waste. My eyes were stinging and I was so busy washing smudges away that my longings, I forgot about. Freshened up and feeling better, I decided the tears were not in vain because my heart was lighter, until the pressure was up again.

The poem ends here, but since it was written about a year ago I believe it is necessary to take it one step further and give God the glory for teaching me that *the tears I shed were an outlet, but if I had my thoughts on Him, the lust of the flesh would not have been a problem.*

As I grew spiritually I learned that when we walk in the spirit, we will not fulfill the lust of the flesh. We can control our thoughts and when we do so we will have the victory if the thoughts are of godly things. **Galatians 5:24,25 "And they that are Christ's have crucified the flesh with the affections and lusts. If we live in the Spirit, let us also walk in the Spirit."**

Longings

Sometimes I lie
All alone
The chesterfield suddenly
Becomes twenty feet long
And an overwhelming urge to cry
Fills my body
My arms cross each other
Hugging my shoulders
In an effort
To comfort
Warm tears fill my eyes
I look to the ceiling
Longing to see a man's eyes
Return my longing
A man's arms hugging me
Instead of my own
The warmth of his body
Instead of a blanket
The sound of his voice

Instead of a record
A man is what I long for
Then, rolling down
The side of my face
'Till it slides into the hole of my ear
Is a tear
My longings for a man
Are overcome
Because off to the bathroom
I run
So busy wiping
This mascara smudged face
No time for self-pity
No time to waste
The longings will return
Another day
For now I am busy
Washing the smudges
Away
Freshened up and feeling better
The tears were not in vain
My heart is now lighter
'Till the pressure's up again

CHAPTER 16

Registration

WITH MY PEN in one hand and my check book in the other I marched up the school steps full of hunger to learn, though it had been years since I last was a student. The song about reading and writing and arithmetic went through my head as I thought about returning to the school where the Golden Rule is taught: *"Do unto others as you would have them do unto you."*

The course I chose to register in was creative writing. Since I had suddenly been writing more and more poetry, and enjoyed it so much I thought it would be a good idea to get some teaching and develop this new-found skill further.

I was determined to retype all the poems I had ever written and take them to school opening night. Like a little kid anxious to show something to the teacher, I had imagined running back to my desk to pray for his approval of my poems after reading them. If he encouraged me as I had hoped he would, I decided I would throw my heart into writing for the rest of my life.

One goal I did have was to make certain credit went where credit was due. I knew any gift I had was a gift from Jesus and wanted him to receive the glory for what he was doing through me. This is the point at which I finished the poem, however, the truth is, I never did take this creative writing course. Allow me to share with you how wonderful Jesus is and how his ways truly are higher than ours.

When I registered for the course I was doing what I thought was the logical thing one does in an effort to improve her skills. BUT, I was looking at the situation from my eyes; Christ's ways are so much higher. He sees the finished product and he knew what was best for me. Consequently, the course was cancelled by the school officials because not enough people registered, and the other high school did not offer this course. God has ways of seeing to it that all these little things are worked out for our good.

Though at the time I was disappointed, I continued to write and the more time that passed, the more hungry I became about writing. Not because I could do great things; I couldn't, but the Holy Spirit is my Guide, my Teacher, my Director, and gives me the words to write. Thus, the more I draw close to the Lord and allow Him to use me for His glory, the more writing He gave me.

How could anyone ever ask for anything else when God, through Jesus, has given us everything we need and more? The most important registration is to see that our name is registered in the Lamb's book of life! **Revelation 20:15 "And whosoever was not found written in the book of life was cast into the lake of fire."**

Registration

With pen in one hand
And check book in the other
I marched up the steps
Into the school
Returning again
To the Golden Rule
The course I have chosen
Is creative writing
I am determined
To go in fighting
The knowledge I yearn
The writing I enjoy
To improve my skills
Is the plot I'll employ
The poems I've written
I shall retype
Then take them to school
On opening night
If I have enough nerve

I'll present them to the teacher
Return to my desk
And pray like a preacher
If my prayers are answered
I'll receive encouragement and praise
Throw my heart into writing
The rest of my days
One goal I have
I'll not lose sight of
Remember the man
In whose light I stand
Any gift I have is from His hand
Credit must go where credit is due
Jesus is the Man
Let Him teach you

CHAPTER 17

Fashion

How WONDERFUL IT is to be able to wear what I want and like, not what some fashion designer insists is right for everyone; and even more wonderful is the fact that I know what is becoming on me, because God has gifted me with spiritual eyes to behold my reflection in the mirror.

One evening I went to a clothing demonstration held at someone's home. It was similar to the jewelry or make-up demonstrations, except this time clothes were being sold. Racks of clothing were hanging on white plastic hangers in the living-room. Several women sat listening to a verbal sales pitch as they looked through a catalogue and price list. Each was as anxious as the next to get their hands on the colorful clothes that were just waiting to be displayed.

When the women were free to look it seemed they each ran and grabbed for the same rack. One hanger was removed; a skirt fell to the floor. Someone held one dress in front of herself, trying to decide, to be or not to be?

Decisions had to be made. Would it be a print, plain, plaid, or floral pattern she chose? Also, which blouse with which skirt? Mix matching clothes is important; maybe a gown would be easier to choose. Then suddenly, this lady's eyes sparkle and she flashes a smile as she reaches for her dream. Flowers all over, with a touch of lace, colors so vivid they lit up her face.

She quickly headed to the change room upstairs. One would think she had no cares. In one minute or so she was completely transformed to an elegant lady serene and reformed. She was so graceful as she descended the staircase, head held high, moving slowly, yet rhythmically with flowers and lace flowing round her figure as she set her pace. She reached the landing, raised one arm high, circled around twice then knelt in a courtesy.

The smooth flowing rhythm was continued as she returned to the top of the staircase, still smiling, still glowing, flowers and lace flowing. This woman was a winner whether she knew it or not. She chose not to purchase on the spot. She wore it, she modeled it, and it boosted her moral. She could easily have left the outfit there, choosing not to purchase anything, yet taking with her an uplifted spirit.

She checked things out; she was thorough before she made up her mind. She did not purchase simply because someone said it looked good or was a good buy. She used a God-given gift, her spiritual eyes. She dressed, then observed from head to toe, the total effect.

Accessories were so very important, yet were overlooked by so many women. She knew the greatest style for her could be ruined by a slip that showed or a run in her pantyhose. She checked not only the clothes, but the hair, make-up, teeth, and nails were all part of the image she gave, so she did not allow a spot check to be sufficient, each detail was scrutinized.

How would an $80.00 dress look if one's nails had polish half off, and an old pair of shoes with the heels worn down, as accessories to compliment? If one has a midriff bulge it would not be wise to draw attention to the bulge by cinching it with a bright red belt, nor would it be wise to wear short skirts if one's legs were fat or discolored because of varicose veins. Granted, she couldn't wear a gown all the time, but the point is she would not be wise in drawing attention to her legs by wearing short skirts, simply because this is what some designer dictates.

When women, WOMEN, begin to look at their total image in the mirror through God's eyes and yield to the changes that should be made, these women will look like ladies, and one will never have a question as to whether one is a male or female! They will also discover how lovely it is to see men begin to act like gentlemen, because *a gentleman knows a lady when he sees one.*

Not only will they look better, these women will feel better, because when you look good, you feel good, and when you feel good, you do well. It is a chain reaction that begins with you. The decision is yours. Do you want to be treated like a lady, the lady you are? If you do, dress like one.

God will give the wisdom you need; to know right from wrong. When He is your fashion designer and co-coordinator you can't go wrong. It is amazing what clothes can do for a gal, when she uses the gift she has been given: spiritual eyes to discern what God's choice is for her.

Fashion

The clothes are hung neatly
On white plastic hangers
The women arrive
With appetites that thrive
On fashion for today
One hanger is removed
The skirt falls to the floor
The size is too small
She hangs it back to the wall
Now a print, or will it be a rose...
Women can't decide
When it comes to clothes
This blouse and that skirt
Or these pants and her top...
Maybe that gown...
But STOP!
Her eyes sparkle and she flashes a smile
As she reaches for her dream
Flowers all over with a touch of lace

Colors so vivid they light up her face
She moves like lightening
To the change room upstairs
Giving the impression
She has absolutely no cares
In less than a minute
She is completely transformed
To an elegant lady
Serene and reformed
So graceful is she
As she descends the staircase
Head held high
Moving slowly yet rhythmically
With flowers and lace
Flowing round her figure
As she sets her pace
She reaches the landing
Raises one arm high
Circles around twice
Then kneels in a curtsey
The smooth flowing rhythm is continued
As she returns to the top of the staircase
Still smiling, still glowing
Flowers and lace
Just flowing
This woman is a winner

Whether she knows it or not
She chose not to purchase
On the spot
She wore it, she modeled it
It boosted her morale
Isn't it amazing what clothes can do
For a gal!

CHAPTER 18

Blackout

How OFTEN IT is that we take things for granted until they are taken away. Then we pine away and regret not appreciating these things when we had them.

One evening I was talking on the phone to a girlfriend while my daughter watched television. Suddenly, there was no longer a picture or sound coming from the television, and all the lights were out. Total blackness because of a power failure. I guided my daughter to the phone so she could hear the warm voice on the other end. As they began to talk to each other, I searched for a candle, a wall, a door, even a door frame; it was totally black.

I slowly followed the wall until my shin and a chair met head on. The silence is gone as an "OUCH" escapes from my mouth. I hobbled about, then pulled open a drawer, smiling as my hand encircles a candle. Then I pick up a pack of matches, only

to discover there is but one left. I said a short but
sincere prayer, asking God to see that this match
would burn and soon the household would be normal again. I made sure I held my breath so as not
to breathe on the flame, thus adding to the difficul-
ties. I struck the match, the wick sent a glow through
the entire room. The glow was light, but somehow
with the light came a warmth too. I breathed a sigh
of relief and my daughter's face reflected a smile of
approval to the light.

Then, amazement was written all over my face because I realized I had no reason whatsoever to be so
concerned over lack of light because the Lord is with
me both day and night.

He was there all the time and He was in control.
Fear is not from Him. He never changes and He has
promised never to leave us or forsake us. He guided
my hands to the candle and match and saw that my
needs were met. He has also promised to supply all
my needs according to His riches in glory, and He
did. Sometimes the things we need most are the little
seemingly unimportant things. They may seem incidental but when God provides and ordains their presence, they are not incidental.

Even more important than the exterior light we see, is the importance of getting our pilot light lit. If you have not asked Jesus into your heart, (He is a Gentleman and won't force His way in) ask Him to forgive your sins, ask Him to be your Savior and Lord, and to take your life and use it for His glory. **Only Jesus can light up your life, and it is an eternal flame He gives, eternal life. You don't have to change batteries at all. He gives only good gifts and this is the greatest gift of all. But it requires commitment and obedience.**

If you are a jogger and have a beautiful body, but your heart is not right with God, your life is worthless. It is the interior that needs to be converted in order to have the balance. Until you receive the spiritual blessings God has for you through His Son, Jesus, the scales will be severely unbalanced, because a suntan, a good figure, a new hairstyle, a new boat or car or home, cannot fulfill a spiritual need. Only Jesus can fill the void. He is standing at your heart's door now and wants to come in. He paid the price for you to have everlasting life. He is looking for disciples.

It is a spiritual battle you are in. **Jesus is bigger than any problem you have.** Make this the hour you decide to be rid of the sin and blackness, as you ask Jesus into your life and let your light shine for Him. From blackout to an eternal flame, eternal life. After all, what have you got to lose? You've tried the devil's ways and not filled the void you seek to fill, now try Jesus. 1John 1:9 "If we confess our sins, he is faithful and just to forgive us our sins and to cleanse us from all unrighteousness."

Blackout

I hear a voice
Talking into the phone
The television is on
A little girl is watching
When suddenly
Total blackness, no picture, no sound
No lights all around
BLACKOUT!

Mother guides daughter
To the phone
Daughter talks to a friend
How warm the voice
At the other end

Mother's arms reach forward
In route for a candle
For a wall

A door frame
ANYTHING at all!

With one hand on the door
She slowly ventures forward
Until she meets HEAD ON
A SHIN to the chair...
The silence is gone
Stars abound everywhere

She hobbles about
Then opens a drawer
Smiles in the darkness
As she touches a candle
Then grasps for matches
Flips open the pack
Alas, there is but one
When will this nightmare be done

She says a prayer
That the match will burn
And soon the household
Will be normal again
Her breath she is holding

Final Request

To prevent a disaster
As she strikes the match
And moves even faster

The wick sends a glow
Through the entire room
She breathes a sigh of relief
As the warmth surrounds her
Amazement is written all over her face

She exclaims aloud
How could I panic
Over lack of light
When the LORD is with me
Day and night!

CHAPTER 19

Death Row

I DROVE HEAD on into a tornado, rather than to a calm sea because as I drove aimlessly down the road... I saw my son standing on the side of the road. It was the first time I had seen him in over one year and I was in a deeper shock upon seeing him unexpectedly.

I braked and stopped my car right in the middle of the road I was so excited, left the car door open and my daughter and I ran to greet him. He was so much taller and such a good-looking boy. In his quiet way, he hugged us and smiled the most precious smile one could ever want to see.

His father was securing a trail bike or dirt bike onto a rack on the car. My son had just finished using it in a field and they were about to leave when I drove by. I really didn't know what to say to him. To be able to just look at him and know he was alive, and well, meant so very much. My eyes absorbed every change in him since I had last seen him. A budding young man really, not a little boy any more.

He grew up so much in one year, and I had not seen him at all. My heart filled with tears over the changes. I had missed. Time cannot be regained. The year had passed and never would I be able to have any memories of he and I sharing that year as a mother and son do because I was not a part of that eventful year with my son.

He also saw changes. I had lost weight and was too thin. My daughter was much taller. They eyed each other and talked like a couple of kittens' eager to play; yet testing each other first. I looked at my husband and the fear that enveloped me was awesome. I remember thinking at that time, "I feel like I'm looking right at the devil." I truly did feel this way. The fear was terrible and very real to me.

I say this because it is a true statement of my feelings. I do not say it to put down my ex-husband. He was unhappy too, this I know, and this book is not to knock anyone down, it is to lift Jesus higher as I tell you what Jesus did.

Since I was going to my parent's house to feed the dog (they were on vacation.) and could not bear to say goodbye to my son after only a few minutes together at the roadside, I asked him to come up to the house (it was only a mile from there) and he could ride his bike in the vacant field next door. It was in a rural area and there just happened to be a trail for dirt bikes through these few acres of land. He and his dad came and it was a day I will never forget. I got on the back of the dirt bike with my son and we went for one bumpy ride and I can assure you I hung on! Not that it was that rough, but I was in a state of shock after receiving a double blow and my nerves had reached the breaking point. Mind you, I didn't hesitate to hug my son because this was something I had wanted to do so many times during the last twelve long months.

As we rode across the field I squealed every now and again, one moment enjoying myself, the next moment scared stiff. It is still music to my ears hearing my son laugh aloud a few times as we rode across the trail, and off the trail too. **He has a good sense of humor and an adventuresome side which he exercised by taking me this route, between apple trees, and over hills as we made our own trail.**

My daughter had several rides with her brother and with her father. I have a couple of enlarged photos of us on the bike, and know it was of God that I was able to have these pictures. To be honest, I had no desire to talk to my husband at all. I did not know the Lord personally at this time, and was still bound with fear and bitterness. He also was not born again. I wanted to see my son again but did not have his address or phone number so I tried to reason with my husband concerning visitation rights (which I do have).

He agreed to bring my son for a dinner a few days later but would not leave him to visit, he insisted on being there too. I wanted to have some privacy with my son, and be able to talk freely but this wasn't possible, so I agreed.

During this two day interim, I shed buckets of tears over my son and over the man I was deceived by. Life seemed so cruel, I began to believe hell was not someplace you go when you die; I believed hell was those events which we experienced living on earth, because I had experienced a living hell for thirteen years. Of course, I know now that there is a hell and a heaven and if we are living in hell.... on earth now, it is because we serve the devil, not God. When we serve God while on earth we become heavenly citizens living on earth (in earthly places) and living a victorious life because we have the power of God working in our life, and when God is on our side we have the majority. Hallelujah. **Psalm 118:6 "The Lord is on my side; I will not fear: what can man do unto me?"**

God was on my side at this time, but I walked away from Him and was doing what I thought was right. He will never leave us or forsake us, this is true. We are the ones who walk away, as did I. When you don't serve God, there is only one other to serve and that is the devil, so I reaped what I sowed, as does everyone.

My daughter and I got out of the car in our apartment parking lot and headed for the apartment. I had sold the house to my parents and moved to an apartment in town. It was Saturday and I planned to prepare dinner soon. Just as I entered the foyer, my son and husband arrived early. My thoughts raced ahead of me. What was the reason they were so early? My husband must be up to something. (How terrible it is when satan attacks your mind.)

You must realize my nerves were so bad I should have been in bed, perhaps even in the hospital at that time. Since I was without a suit of armor to protect myself spiritually, as I wrote about earlier, the devil attacked front, left, and center with every bit of ammunition he had. Fear was the biggest weapon he used.

I had thought that my husband was trying to kill me when I was in the hospital just a few months after we separated, and this fear had never left. I also had a dreadful fear of guns because of things that happened in our marriage concerning guns, and needed deliverance from this fear.

The fear was eating away at my mind daily as satan, the devourer robbed me more and more of peace. **John 10:10 "The thief cometh not, but for to steal, and to kill, and to destroy: I am come that they might have life, and that they might have it more abundantly."**

My son and husband entered the foyer and I reached for my key to open the inner door. Then I saw it, my husband was holding something in his hands. A green garbage bag was wrapped around it and the shape was long and thin like a rifle. **I truly believed it was a rifle and he was going to kill me.** I said, **"What's that?"**

He said, **"Oh it's a surprise."** *"I was horrified and I thought, A surprise, yeah, you'll get me upstairs to the apartment then you're going to kill us."* He and both kids were still standing waiting for me to unlock the inner door. I couldn't move, but said, *"It's a gun isn't it. I know it's a gun."* It was his turn to be shocked at that point, and he was.

For the first time, I believe it registered in his heart the mental damage that had been done to me over the years by his obsession with guns and the threats, etc. His face registered shock, then compassion for the first time. *(The gun threats began three months after we were married and I believed he would do what he said.)* **He knew my fear was very real. He quickly denied that it was a gun, and handed it to my son.** *This upset me even more because I thought he must have turned my son against me and my son was going to use the gun to kill my daughter and me.*

At that very moment, something inside my stomach and chest included... just shattered

to bits as if the trigger had been pulled. I felt that if I put my hand to my stomach there would be a big hole and I could put my hand right through it. I was dead, but didn't die, dead, but I didn't fall.

My mind slowed to almost stop, no fight left, all desire to live had been snuffed out of my life. I heard voices saying, "Open the door." Automatically, I opened the door and began the long ascent up a high wide staircase. (I lived over a plaza in a new apartment and there was a long steep staircase to climb, with one landing half-way up.)

I was first, but not for long, soon the children and my husband passed me on the stairs, then stood at the top waiting for me. Each step I took was more difficult than the first. With each step, my feet became heavier and heavier until I could have sworn they were covered in concrete, weighing me down.

My life flashed by me in a minute and the only thing that really mattered was my children. They were all I lived for. I really didn't care about myself. They were my everything. I had shed tears together with my daughter many times as we drew closer through the heartbreak of separation. Yet, the tears did not bring my son home, and now, it would be over in a matter of minutes.

I recalled newspaper headlines where this kind of murder/suicide had actually happened and now thought it would be my family, not some family I didn't know, that would-be victims of such a fate. As I tried so hard to climb the stairs, it felt like some force I could not see was literally holding me back, pushing against me as I tried even harder to climb. It was so strong, so powerful, and so frightening, but I forced my way to the top until I made it.

I opened the door at the top of the stairs and began the final walk down the long hall to my apartment: I saw death row. There was a red carpet on the hall floor and about ten big dome lights in the ceiling spaced out down the full length of the hall past the other apartments. I began what seemed a very long walk. The only difference between this and the movies was that the movies show the gas chamber or the electric chair at the end of the hall, at the end of death row. My death would not be at the end of the hall, but in the apartment. (These were my thoughts).

As I walked I imagined prisoners behind each apartment door I passed, because although I knew I was in my apartment building, I was also positive these were my last moments to live and the other tenants could not help me at all. They were as helpless to me as prisoners in other cells would be when one walks down death row.

As I passed by some doors I recalled hearing arguments and swearing; parties with the drinking going on until all hours and buried deep within me somewhere, was the knowledge that these people were no better off than me. They were in the same kind of hell, so there was no point in calling on them. I continued on down the hall, the lights seemed very bright.

Then I saw my children's faces as they looked at each other with such love, totally oblivious to what was about to happen. I began to sob uncontrollably. Finally, I opened the apartment door and stepped inside, at the same time hoping it would be fast, one, two, three blasts: over with soon!

My thoughts did not go to heaven or hell. I think I really believed the hell I had lived was about to end, and now I would have peace. My desire to live was no lon-ger a desire. I sat in the living-room sobbing and wait-ing, imagining pools of blood all over the white rug. I could not talk, only look at the others, as I waited for the end to come. I thought my husband was just try-ing to get his nerve up as he looked around nervously.

My son was naturally upset by my tears, not under-standing why I was so moved. I couldn't explain. I held him and said, **"It's just that I'm so glad to see you." My daughter was very affectionate too and their af-fection and concern was tearing me apart even more since it was their love I had wanted more than any-thing in the world, and now we were together, but we could not enjoy each other because we were about to die. My heart could never have been in more pieces than it was at that moment. An arrow couldn't have pierced it because the pieces were too small.**

The green garbage bag was unwrapped and there was not a rifle inside. It was a large frozen fish. It was so long it would not fit in my freezer and there was a large refrigerator in the apartment. Granted, I was relieved it was not a rifle, yet puzzled because I could not understand why my husband came if it was not to kill us. **At this point it really didn't matter that it**

wasn't a gun because the damage had already been done mentally and emotionally.

It was only by the grace of God that I managed to prepare and serve dinner but I don't even remember what I served. **I do remember my son asking for a second helping of dessert (I had cooked apples with tea biscuits on top) and he couldn't have said anything to make me happier. I will never forget his hesitancy to ask, and the twinkle in his eye when he did.**

Later, I took pictures of the kids eating donuts filled with whipped cream and the few pictures I took, I now treasure because they are the most recent I have.

I've not seen him at all in the three and a half years following. Prior to this I saw him once, then once more a full year later. So there is a period of four and a half years when I have not seen my son at all, yet I have visitation rights.

One very beautiful moment I had with my son that day was the only time he and I were alone for a few minutes. I asked him if he ever wore the little gold cross I had given him on his birthday fifteen months earlier.

He said, **"I wore it so much I broke the chain."** I was so uplifted when he said this. It gave me some of the strength I needed at this particular time. The Bible says in **Nehemiah 8:10 "... for The joy of the Lord is your strength."** **His words brought joy to my heart and I was strengthened.**

I reached into my jewelry box and picked up a necklace he had given me when he and his dad returned from Florida after living there a few months. The gold chain had an ivory pendant with two gold palm trees on it and I treasured it, and still do. I took the chain off and gave it to him to use to put his cross on so he could wear it. **He beamed and I was delighted too. It seemed a special bond drawing us together.**

> *From the experience I have shared with you, can you understand how we make our own life a hell on earth when we do not put God first, thus allowing the devil to pick at our minds?* *I don't think I can say much else that makes it clear how important it is to stop trying to find a magic solution; a storybook fairytale becoming reality; a solution to your problems through sex, booze, drugs, divorce, and running away from problems.*

The only way to solve your problems is to meet them head on. When you serve God there will be no fear. Perfect love casteth out all fear. **1John 4:18 "There is no fear in love, but perfect love casteth out fear; because fear hath great torment. He that feareth is not made perfect in love."**

Face the fact that a lot of your own unhappiness is not someone else's fault, it is yours. Don't blame others for your own shortcomings. You are the one that made the decision to be on the road you are on, so don't blame anyone else. No one forced you to do anything. God gave you a mind to use and a free will, the same as everyone else. How about giving back to him some of the love he has given you? How about accepting the gifts Christ has already paid for? Jesus is the answer to whatever your problem may be.

Talk to him now, you'll see. Don't just take it from me. He knows your hurt and despair and he is always there. His power is greater than any other. Allow your problems to throw you right into the arms of Jesus and you won't have any more problems, they'll be His.

He said in **Matthew 11:30 "For my yoke is easy, and my burden is light."** Bring all your needs to the altar, to the Lord, he can help you and is willing and able. God is able and God does all things well!

Death Row

How would you feel
If your final sentence had been received
And you walked toward the end of the hall
Grieved

Would you rejoice
Knowing you would not be going to hell
Or would you be under strain where you are going
Along with an attitude of, "Oh well."

Perhaps you would shake and scream and cry
With each step you took
Or perhaps you would pray
As in your shoes you shook

You might refuse to walk
Forcing someone to carry you
Or would you obey as usual
Because that is the thing to do

Would the love of Jesus, the glory of the Lord
Shine in your face
As you walked with a sure
And steady pace

What would your final request be
As you walked down death row
Think about it
Jesus wants to know

CHAPTER 20

Frying Pan

THIS PARTICULAR POEM and story is something I did not want to put in my book nor did I want to write about it all. God has been preparing me to write about this even though I must admit I did not yield quickly or easily.

There are certain experiences in my past life, when I was serving satan, that I do not want to think about at all, and I am still ashamed and embarrassed of what I did. It doesn't seem possible that what I am going to reveal to you was actually a part of my life. The only way I am able to write about it is because God has totally forgiven me of ALL my sins, and forgotten those sins. Actually, I am not ashamed or embarrassed anymore because God changed me. *That Linda died.*

I write the following not to flaunt any sin, but to show what a wonderful God I serve and how He changed me. No names, or specific details are given because I don't believe I have to lift satan before I can lift Jesus. I will tell you enough to give you a clear picture of the kind of life I used to live, thus enabling you to see where God has brought me from and what He has done through me. The only reason I share the past experiences is so God will receive full glory for what He has done for me.

It is only because of the Holy Spirit convicting me that I am about to dive deep into the pit as I go on a trip down memory lane, into the past when I walked not a narrow road to heaven, but a wide common road to hell as I served the devil, satan. I have prayed that each and every person I met when I was not serving God, will read this book from cover to cover and as the truth touches your heart you reach out and becomes a born again Spirit filled Christian and walk the same beautiful narrow goal paved road that I am now on. A short number of months on hell's highway seems like an eternity. Yet God gave everyone a free will and thankfully, He lifted me to His heart of love and I do not look back.

Please bear with me as I insert a special note to my son whom I have not seen for over two years: *Son, Since God has taught me to keep my eyes on Him and not on my problems, I must write what He has inspired me to write. I pray that you read the entire book, don't stop reading. Allow God to show you what He has done for me and how He has changed me in so many beautiful and necessary ways. There were a lot of things wrong with me and I'm still not perfect, but God is on my side and (Mark 10:27 "With God all things are possible.) so I pray that through this book you will reach a deeper understanding of what I went through... and you will release any bitterness and allow God to replace it with love as He ministers to you through what I've written.*

If this book results in you and I being able to see each other and restoring our relationship as a mother/ son relationship should be, then to God be the glory, and it will have been worth opening all the wounds that had to be opened and cleansed in order to write it. Not only are they opened, but God cleansed each wound and healed me completely. I can write only because God has strengthened me. Please remember one thing, I long to see you and I love you with all my heart, as does your sister and Grammie, Grandpop and your Uncle. Our prayers are lifted for you daily and I know we will be together soon.

You can contact me at the address in the book and I pray you do.

It is time that hole in my heart was mended and you can mend it. I'm sure you remember our conversation. Your sister and I will be complete when our love for you is also returned through you to us. May God bless you and everyone that reads this book.

Love, Mom xoxo

At this point in my life I had become a born again Christian by giving my life to Jesus and asking forgiveness of all my sins, but I did not yet know what it meant to be born again. I had no real understanding of what had happened to me spiritually because I was not going to church, nor did I know anyone who was a born again Christian, or if I did, they did not let their light shine.

You see, when I gave my life to Jesus, my inner man, my old nature changed and I become a new creation. Now, my desires changed because I was saved and God was giving me the desire to do what He wanted me to do. It wasn't as if I was having a hard time to quit smoking or drinking, because He took the desire to do so away. He delivered me from cigarettes after and eighteen-year habit and I lost any desire to drink alcoholic beverages.

Now...........I was a threat to satan because I was no longer on his wide road to hell, I was on the narrow road to heaven. He knows he is going to hell and he wants to take as many people with him as possible.

So what does one do when one's prisoner escapes? One attacks. What happens when the enemy attacks and you are not armed? The enemy gains control because you are defenseless. The reason I was defenseless is because although I decided to follow Jesus, I was not reading the Bible or attending church to be fed spiritually. I don't even carry a gun but that is not the kind of armor I am talking about.

I am talking about spiritual armor (I do carry a spiritual gun, the Word of God in my heart now, it is alive and powerful and loaded at all times) because it is a spiritual battle we are in. Now, absorb this fact.

You are accustomed to seeing battles and fights on the television, in movies, and on some streets and alleys, but the physical fighting you see is only the surface of a much deeper battle. It is a spiritual battle we are in and we need to be aware of this at all time. This applies to everyone in the whole world whether they are saved or not.

In the New Testament Ephesians chapter six, verse eleven through nineteen teach us how to put on the armor we need. Verse twelve reads: "For we wrestle not against flesh and blood, but against principalities, against powers, against the rulers of the darkness of this world, against spiritual wickedness in high places. Verse thirteen reads, "Wherefore take unto you the whole armour of God, that ye may be able to withstand in the evil day, and having done all, to stand."

I wore no armor at all, and because I had been attending what is referred to as a dead church in my childhood years and some in the following years, I did not think I would find the answer in church. This is why I looked elsewhere for fulfillment, while at the same time, trying to talk to God, who seemed miles away, but I kept trying to establish a relationship with Him.

All that God gives us is good. Self-pity, depression, worry, and loneliness are just a sample of what satan gives you. I wallowed in all of this until the loneliness I could no longer cope with. I was almost totally abandoned by those that were friends and acquaintances when I was married.

They had a way of disappearing or simply being too busy to call. Sometimes a wife considered me a threat to her marriage (which was obviously already in difficulty or she would never have even thought this). She would have been secure about her relationship with her husband regardless of whether I knew them or not. Other people were uncomfortable in my presence, they didn't know what to say or do, so many came once or twice, then stopped. Others observed but did not call.

Yet others talked and talked and talked, not to me, but about me! (If the shoe fits...) Through it all I learned what a hell loneliness is. I was so desperate to have friends who were sincere, I needed someone to talk to other than my parents. They were such a help to me, completely supportive at all times, even through their own heartbreak of not seeing their grandson.

Nevertheless, I needed someone my own age to visit with. I had been separated one and a half years, taken a refresher course at college, was working full time now at secretarial work so my days were busy, but evenings were like mountains ahead of me. My divorce was final in less than six months after this period of time, and I was in no hurry to get married after being so hurt.

Instead, I avoided marriage, and got hurt even more by going from the frying pan right into the fire. Someone told me about a group that met once a week at a church. They were all separated or divorced, and got together to visit, play cards, games, sometimes they invited a speaker, and there were special events for the children too on scheduled week-ends. This sounded really good, and since most, not all, of my married friends abandoned me I decided these people would understand how I felt because they were in the same boat at some time so I arranged to go with a friend.

This was the beginning of a whole new world opening up to me but what seemed like good intentions did not stop there. I am not pointing the finger at any club, I realize all are free to come and go as they please, we all have a free will and I exercised mine when I chose to go. I do think this kind of club is very harmful for people who are in such vulnerable positions and consequently the club is an open door for further heartbreak and grief.

I think it is important to point out the fact that putting lonely people of the opposite sex together is like putting magnets face to face and expecting them not to be drawn to each other. (Not to mention the fact that this group was not a Christian group, so there were no morals to line up with the Word of God.) Temptation was about as plentiful as weeds in a garden at the peak of summer.

In a desperate search to fill lonely hours I became one of the crowd. Anyone can be one of a crowd. What happened to me is certainly not an original story, because I can name many others that followed the same pattern. Many of them are still in the same pit still groping in a life of phoniness and deception as they seek an answer for the peace and true love they want, but will never find in the pit of hell.

Others know Jesus but have backslid because they did not draw the strength from Him that they need. They yielded to temptation, and they can't blame God because God never allows us to be tempted beyond that which we are able, but will make a way to escape. I know because I have learned to resist temptation and take the way of escape God offers. **First Corinthians 10:13 Living Bible (TLB) "But remember this-the wrong desires that come into your life aren't anything new and different. Many others have faced exactly the same problems before you. And no temptation is irresistible. You can trust God to keep the temptation from becoming so strong that you can't stand up against it, for he has promised this and will do what he says. He will show you how to escape temptation's power so that you can bear up patiently against it.**" *That's the Bible... folks. Pretty clear, isn't it?!*

At the time, I began to attend these meetings it was a different story. God was not in control of my life then. I, self, sat on the throne of my heart. God will not violate anyone's free will; the decision to do my own thing was mine. I simply followed the crowd.

After the meeting was over many of the members met at a local bar, often referred to as the dungeon, or the den of iniquity. How true, and if only I had

listened to those words and absorbed their mean-
ing. It was very dimly lit, supposedly romantic, ac-
companied with loud rock music. Bottom line, a
bar, a dungeon.

I never did like beer or the taste of liquor but now I
was one of the gang, so I ordered along with the rest.
What began with one drink soon resulted in three
drinks in an evening. My grocery money paid for
them, and one mid-week meeting was not enough, we
began to come to the bar on the week-end too. Soon
there were times when we skipped the club meetings
and just went to the bar, as did some others from the
club.

The devil allowed us to believe we were having a
good time because we weren't sitting home alone,
and we were with all these people. Then the evening progressed, as did the effects of the alcohol,
and soon I was in someone's arms dancing to a beat
I didn't even hear because it felt so good to have
someone's arms around me.

A conversation was not easy to have because the music
was so loud. (This is another of the devil's ways to
prevent people from opening up and being honest.)

When you have to yell, it's a little difficult to yell facts about being separated, etc. and not become inhibited because of having to talk so loudly. So, I drank and smoke and danced until it was closing time. Often, I drove several girls home, sometimes less in number than I drove to the meeting.

The lust of the flesh won the battle and another door was opened. Lust produces consequences - what you sow, you shall reap. With fornication is far more than sexual sin. Ungodly soul ties are formed and particles of the person's soul are taken. **There always is a price to pay for sin... it is called "death, spiritual death".**

The devil does not get the credit or blame for all my sins. I had a free will the same as you have and I chose to look for love. I was searching for something I had not yet found. It was like a treadmill with no end, no purpose, until I realized I was telling myself I was having a good time because I wasn't sitting home alone. **If you are having a good time you'll know it, you won't have to tell yourself you are!** I was trying to convince myself, yet at the same time, I did not know how to use the power we have through Jesus since I was not receiving the teaching I needed. The Bible says to submit to God, resist the devil and he will flee. You resist him, not in your own power, but in the Name of Jesus. That is work. It is called spiritual warfare. I needed to get with it and not compromise.

I would use grocery money for liquor to entertain; I was so desperate to have friends and be popular and needed. Such a cry for help!! I was more de- pressed than when the evening had begun because this is another of the effects alcohol has on you. You never stay high; you get high, then lower than you were when you started. People do not talk about this though.

It is just another way in which the devil has led so many down the wide road to hell. And I did not even like booze of any kind. It was a tool to 'be like the crowd'. Of what? Losers. Dance the night away and not even hear the song lyrics. No one was focused on God. The flesh, the carnal nature was in control.

I felt like an arrow being pushed wrongly, by some unseen force. Each week I became more and more unhappy. If you see someone that might fit the shoes I was in, don't criticize them, or be disgusted with them. Pray for them, because they are really very unhappy people and they need our prayers. **Anyone can knock**

them down. Separate from the crowd and lift them up in prayer. God used four people to help me get free from hell's grip. The mind is the battleground, fear, torment, lack, poverty, loneliness, rejection, betrayal, depression, are all tools of satan and since it was not God I was sold out to, I suffered unmercifully. As did others. But God positioned some people to help me. Plus I found out an aunt who visited from Oregon, had put me on her prayer list, there were 2,000 in the congregation and that is why my hell got stopped short. Thank God!

One was a man who taught school at a training school for juveniles where I worked in the office. He told me about a miracle service that was being held on two different occasions, and who the speaker was. But I did not really understand that this was the power of God working. I had been so involved in the occult I thought it was something to do with that, not the power of God. So, I did not attend. Plus, I could not figure out why a preacher was going to the high school gym, not a church. **To my carnal mind, it sounded like he was lost.**

The second laborer to plant a seed was a Dutch lady who was a born-again Spirit filled Christian. She was a friend of a friend of mine who decided that when I kept talking about the Lord, and got "religious" (as she put it), that she would introduce me to her friend who was "very religious"! **Talk about birds of a feather flocking together! She just knew we had something in common, and she was right, but it was not a religious spirit, it was JESUS.**

We were both born again and this woman came to my home and spent the entire evening talking about Jesus. It was the first time in my life I ever talked about Jesus all night and wasn't embarrassed to do so, and didn't want to talk about anything else either. *I had wasted enough years with foolish small talk. This woman even rode a bicycle to come to minister to me and this touched my heart.* **She ministered the love of Jesus to me and I was drawn to Jesus more and more.**

I was like a very dry sponge being exposed to water and was ready to absorb that special water, the living water only He can give us. She was so patient and gentle with me, not pushy at all, a real Saint. She had to repeat things and knew my nerves were not good, yet she was so patient and understanding with me.

We said a prayer together, and it was the first time in my life anyone ever prayed with me as we stood together and held hands and prayed. Something happened, but I didn't know what. (Now I know it was the power and presence of God I felt in my own apartment.) She told me to feel free to phone her at any hour, and we agreed to meet again. We did on two occasions, briefly at her home, and other friends were there. Once it was on Halloween. Then there was a second time when I phoned her and we arranged for her to come over that night at 7:30.

When 7 P.M. arrived, I had such a headache I could hardly stand up, and a pain in my chest. The pain in my chest was so severe I could only breathe short gasps of air, and finally phoned her because I didn't know if I would be able to visit if this continued. We talked and she asked me when it started. I remember telling her it started not long after we talked on the phone earlier and she agreed to come over. Little did I know this made it very clear to her who she had to bind and cast out. This pain was sure not from God, it was one of the enemy's tactics to prevent her from letting her light shine.

Praise God, because she came and visited, shared, I asked questions and remember taking notes too. I remember her telling me there was a price to pay if I chose to serve the Lord, and that it was a serious decision to be made, not to be taken lightly. I shied away a bit as far as making a full commitment, said I would think about it, but did agree to pray with her. When she said the word 'Lord" I thought of Robin Hood, a program my brother used to watch on television, when we were kids and it had something to do with Lords, so I pulled back; but I did want Jesus.

She told me about how God would deliver me from cigarettes and what to pray. I wrote this down, and was definitely interested. This point really sunk the hook deeper into my heart because I hated the taste the smoke put in my mouth, not to mention the damage it could do, but was not able to quit on my own. She was led by the Holy Spirit and I am so thankful to her for leading me as she did at that time.

The third laborer was a woman I hired to work for me while I was managing a jug milk store. I had hired many different women, but this one was very different. She made no bones about telling me of her involvement in what she considered a very upstanding religious group.

She told me about a big convention coming up that was out of town, and agreed to work as many hours as I needed her because she was saving to go to this fantastic convention. Her face lit up when she talked about it and I wondered why I didn't feel like that when I thought of Jesus. As far as her religion was concerned I was taught that the group she was with was a cult.

However, this did not hinder me from hiring her because I didn't care what her religious beliefs were. All I wanted was a trustworthy good worker. **She always managed to somehow start talking about Jesus.** It didn't seem to matter what I said, she knew how to bring Him into the conversation. It was uncanny. There were times I thought she would drive me nuts. It was most disturbing.

I remember cleaning cans and shelves, and she was talking so openly, so freely, so unashamedly about Jesus. I would look over to the door and hope no one came into the store while she was talking about Jesus. I was concerned that they might not come back again if they thought we were preaching to them.

She sure was a thorn to me, but I know now in fact, a great blessing because my thoughts didn't stray much when she was there, and the Holy Spirit had a lot of chances to convict me as well as plant seeds as she witnesses. She was simply letting here light shine and this is what we are called to do. I now pray she is no longer in a cult.

During this time in my life, the Dutch lady was the only one that said things to me that really made me believe that Jesus just might love ME. I would sing that song, **"Jesus Loves Me"** and play it on the organ at home, and cry because somehow in my heart, **I knew He loved me, but I didn't KNOW him and I couldn't seem to find Him.**

As the Bible says, **Hosea 4:6 "My people are destroyed for lack of knowledge…"** I was a perfect example. Don't ever hesitate to tell someone **"Jesus Loves You"**, you will never know the good that is done and the hope this brings to someone.

The fourth laborers were a couple of charismatic Christians named Pat Robertson and Ben Kinchlow from the 700 Club on television. I discovered this program quite by accident, at least I thought it was by accident.

I thought it was a game show when I read the name in the television guide. It was through this program that I became convicted and began to see realistically concerning my immoral behavior. **Cobwebs were pulled away from my eyes as I watched the program, but didn't want to watch.**

Of course, you know who did not want me to watch it, the devil. I couldn't seem to turn it off though. I remember hearing Ben say, **"Praise the Lord!",** yet I didn't absorb much more of the program than that at first. I was so tired from work I just lay there listening.

Then there came a time when I remember thinking as I lay on the chesterfield, **"If that guy says praise the Lord one more time, I'll put my foot right through the television."** He did, and I didn't, my television is still intact. Praise the Lord!

God was trying so hard to help me. I remember sitting in the bar and I just knew it was God that allowed me to see the people through His eyes. The pretty faces and bodies, handsome men, were no longer pretty or handsome. They wore masks over the saddest, most empty, expressionless faces. Their eyes revealed the most... confusion, desperation, death. *The eyes are the mirrors to your soul and this is true. No amount of make-up can disguise the truth.* I saw people trying so hard to have a good time. It was pathetic.

I stopped dancing and became more interested in observing people. They would not admit the truth about how they felt. They were so phony. I pointed the finger, yet I still went. I was in my thirties at this time and I think it is important to point out that so many of the people that followed the very same route as I did, were so very young, in their twenties even. How very unhappy they must be to have plunged into sin at such a young age.

I would not want to live as a teenager in this day and age, (and not be saved). I believe one reason we see so much sin and violence among the youth of today is because the parents are not teaching according to Scripture. They don't have time for God. Going to church means you can't sleep in. That's right, but, when you go to church and allow God to come into your life, you won't want to sleep in because He will give you the desire to do what He wants you to do. Commitment costs.

So many people tend to shy away from churches because they think they will have to live up to some standard set by Miss or Mrs. Goody two shoes. Not so. I could never stop smoking, drinking, illicit sex, and clean up my act myself. In my own strength, this was not possible. It is not possible for anyone else to do it either and live as God wants him/her to, unless he/she had given their life to the Lord and asked the Holy Spirit to fill him/her and then that person will have the power of God working in their life and be able to become the person God made him/her to be.

The Holy Spirit gives the power to love with God's unconditional love. The Holy Spirit, not you, does the inner work necessary to make you more like Christ. This is what is meant when we say, "Let go and let God." We make things so complicated when God has made them so easy. **Acts 1:8 "But ye shall receive power after that the Holy Ghost is come upon you: and ye shall be witnesses unto me..."**

The word love is so misused and abused. If people were freed from the spirit of lust there would be thousands of people that would soon realize they do not "love" their common-law spouses, and in some cases their husband/wife, because they have

never known true love. There is a world of difference in love and lust.

I did not love the people and knew they did not love
me. I saw turned off feelings to protect from more
hurt yet that is not a solution to avoid pain. Robots crying out for love yet responding with locked emotions.

Shopping centers housed many people, unsmiling
faces whose eyes searched for an answer. I reached
a point when I had to face reality and the reality was:
I was not at all happy. I didn't even like myself, let
alone others, except for my family.

I had made things complicated to the degree that I
could not cope any longer with things as they were.
I reached the point called **"Wit's End"**. I was literally at my wits' end, and am so thankful to God
that He kept people with drugs away from me, and
I was spared from that pit; and I was not seriously
suicidal (I was not going to do anything drastic, although I did want to die). This is when I turned to
the only answer.

**I returned home alone one night, knelt beside my
bed and cried buckets. I cried and cried and cried**

and tried to remember every sin I ever committed and asked God to forgive me. Then I prayed for each person I even talked to let alone was involved with, I prayed for their salvation.

Next, I told God I needed to know Him better and I would go to church in an effort to try and get on the right track. Also, I promised to stay away from the bar, singles dances, singles clubs, and the people I had been chumming with because their morals were no better than mine and I was determined to do everything I could in an effort to get right with God and find peace. *This was the first real commitment I made to God except as a child.*

> *When my friends missed me, and began to phone I witnessed effectively from this point on because I was living a holy life for the first time, and stuck to my commitment I made to God. I discovered a new boldness to speak about Jesus that I had never known before. The more I talked about Him the more excited I got and the more I wanted to talk about Him even more. It was beautiful and exciting, as were some of the reactions of those I witnessed to.*

I found myself suddenly able to quickly find an opening to share Jesus with someone on the phone. Not only was I surprised to be able to do this, I was even more surprised when people listened. They had a freedom to talk on the phone that they would not have had if we were in person. They asked questions and I was surprised to hear some of the answers because I didn't know I knew some of those things that I said. *Soon I was as interested in what I was saying, as I was in what they were saying in response. God was in it. This was the wisdom of God coming through me as I yielded to Him. These were His words and I was just the vessel. What a glorious revelation it was for me! That God could actually use me.*

2 Corinthians 4:5-7 The Living Bible (TLB)
"We don't go around preaching about ourselves but about Christ Jesus as Lord. All we say of ourselves is that we are your slaves because of what Jesus has done for us. For God, who said, "Let there be light in the darkness." has made us understand that it is the brightness of his glory that is seen in the face of Jesus Christ. But this precious treasure-this light and power that now shine

within us is held in a perishable container, that is, in our weak bodies. Everyone can see that the glorious power within must be from God and is not our own."

I did not care when some friends laughed and some didn't believe I was serious, because many listened. Then others phoned because of what was said in a previous call with someone else. They had relayed my conversation to them and this person then had to phone and find out first hand.

That was fine with me because I got another chance to talk about Jesus. Soon people realized I was really serious and *my best way of witnessing was by not being at the place I used to frequent. They talked and they had to talk about Jesus because they knew Jesus was the reason I was not there with them.*

I told them I had turned over a new leaf, and then explained further. They agreed that they were not happy or they would not be phoning me. I told them I faced the fact that sex, booze and cigarettes were not the answer and I had FOUND the answer. Then I told them I had tried the road they were on and knew already it was not the answer, so I asked them to try the road I was on that led to heaven with Jesus. Questions were asked and God was faithful in giving me the right answers, because I sure didn't have all of the answers.

Although I knew it was the Lord giving me wisdom and speaking through me, I did not yet understand how He was doing this because it was my voice and my mouth, yet His words. That's okay though because God knew exactly how I felt and He knew where to lead me so I would get the teaching I needed. Praise the Lord.

When the phone calls continued, temptation that used to be temptation was just not there anymore although it was the same people phoning. **I now had a desire to be a godly woman. It was as simple as that. I didn't do a thing except put my trust in God and meant what I said when I made a commitment to serve Him. He revealed himself to me many different ways.**

On one occasion when I was witnessing by phone to a man who was very angry to think I was actually serious about Jesus, he did everything he could to try to convince me that everything the Bible said was not true. He said, "Then if what you say is true, how come when I saw a picture of Adam, he had a belly button, if he was made by God?"

Immediately, I answered, *"I didn't know they had cameras then."* He hung up. He did call one more time and I was able to say a little more but he was not ready to make a commitment. If we wait until we understand everything, we will wait forever, because we are not capable of understanding it all. We need the Holy Spirit to dwell in us to give us the understanding we are looking for. **Isaiah 55:8-9 "For my thoughts are not your thoughts, neither are your ways my ways, saith the Lord. For as the heavens are higher than the earth, so are my ways higher than your ways, and my thoughts than your thoughts."**

The answer is really so simple. We are the ones who make it complicated. I don't know of anyone that ever won an argument with God, and rightly so. Who are we to question Him? Does the pot argue with its maker? *We should be so thankful that God is so patient and understanding.*

One woman I witnessed to said, **"That's okay for you, but I don't have that much faith so I can't believe like you do."** *Hogwash!!! That is just an excuse to justify not making a commitment.* I know because I felt the same way before. I thought I had to get my act cleaned up, then I would be good enough to be a Christian. If that were true, none of us would ever be a Christian because we can't do GOD'S work. No way will we ever be able to do his job.

He will do his work in and through us, but only if we yield and let Him have his way, for He knows what is best. He loves each of us more than we could ever imagine. No matter how many problems we have, we must realize that Jesus is closer than any problem and has the answer for each one. **Matthew 17:20 "… If ye have faith as a grain of mustard seed, ye shall say unto this mountain, Remove hence to yonder place; and it shall remove; and nothing shall be impossible unto you."**

As far as the church was concerned, after two weeks passed I went to a service at the denominational church I had attended as a kid. I attended services Sunday morning for four Sundays in a row. The first Sunday I remember the preacher talking about Moses and saying, **"Who knows, we may even have a Moses here in this congregation."** My eyes filled with tears and I did not know why.

This statement really got me thinking, but the following three Sundays I did not receive anything to fill the void and I was listening to every word because I was hungry to learn. There was no sinner's prayer for the unsaved. There was no altar call. No one prayed with me, I shook hands with a lot of sober faced people and that was the extent of any contact. The love of Jesus was still something I was searching for.

The only other moment that touched my heart was when a woman in the choir sang a solo: **"Did you remember to pray today?"** Excellent, but as for the sermon, I was bored and unmoved. It was a dead church. When I returned home I was in tears because I believed I felt the presence of God in my home, yet not in church! I couldn't understand this. **If I couldn't find God in church; WHERE WAS HE???!!!**

I felt frustrated, tearful, lonely and confused after six weeks had passed and the phone stopped ringing, and there were no visitors, I was as good as **"under quarantine"**.

I was very happy with my daughter and content to stay home and be with her, but after six weeks of such isolation, loneliness took hold. I did something I had never done. I was so sick of sitting home every week night and every week-end I went to a singles dance alone. That is the last dance that I have ever attended too, because something happened at that dance that was the final step to getting me on the right track once and for all!

There were long tables on the outside walls of the room, each one seating about twenty people. I entered the dance hall and sat at one of their tables where only about five other people were seated. There was one woman near me that came alone and we began to talk, then we went to get a drink. When we returned to our table there was a man sitting in the seat right next to mine.

I was infuriated, "Who did he think he was to sit right there, there were all kinds of seats.....he didn't have to sit here. Now everyone will think I am with him and no one will ask me to dance. Of all the nerve!" I tried to ignore him and debated moving to another table but didn't. He asked me to dance and I danced a few dances then sat down. He still came back to the same table too. I got another drink and came back to the table. I noticed he was only drinking pop, not liquor but didn't say anything. Without realizing it I think I felt better about it because I knew drinking and driving does not mix and thought this was one less person who would be a highway hazard. I was impressed, but would not tell him so.

He asked someone else to dance and I danced with others too but we still came back to the same table. He asked if I came there very often. I told him I had not been there for six weeks and did not know why I was there that night. I was even shocked at the truthfulness and boldness with which I spoke. **I was truthful before, but not so open to admit I was not happy, (before there was a mask, but not any more).**

He looked at me and said he could take me somewhere the following day where he guaranteed I would have a good time. I didn't even answer him because I was so sick of hearing so many lines from others that I didn't even pretend to be polite. I was not looking for a boyfriend. I was not even sure why I was there.

Then a little later in the evening he said it again, **"I could take you somewhere tomorrow that I guarantee you would have a good time."** BUT, THIS TIME when he said it, his face lit up and he absolutely glowed. I had never seen this happen to anyone before. I decided I better find out where this place is if it can make him light up like that.

Quickly I was trying to figure out what is open on Sunday and wondered about stock car races, bowling, and couldn't see that these events would cause him to look like he did. He told me the name of the church he would take me to and I said I couldn't go because my daughter was singing in the choir at home for the first time. He was so surprised he hit me in the shoulder with his fist, half gently, and shouted out loud, **"Are YOU a CHRISTIAN?"** Well, I was ready to lambaste this guy for being so loud and especially for being so surprised. After all, I had considered myself a Christian for years, so I was quite indignant about his question. I said, **"YES!!"** He looked at me, then at the drink of rye in my hand and said, **"Well you would never know it!!"**

I sat there as the words pierced my heart, and never did finish the drink nor have I had a drop since, praise God. **I was so convicted!** We talked further and exchanged phone numbers. The following Sunday he took my daughter and I out for dinner, then to a church service where the power of God was so strong, as I share in the poem "Praise the Lord".

It was at that time I truly became born again and had the power of God working in my life and the teaching I needed was received. **I was taken from the frying pan into the fire by the devil and then**

introduced to the fire of the Holy Ghost by the grace of God. Hallelujah. If you don't know what this is, read on, because the best is yet to come. You need to read all of the book to get the entire picture because it is so important that God receives the glory for all that He has done.

I have learned that experience can be a great teacher! One thing of interest is the fact that many men accuse their wives of not being able to satisfy them sexually. It is easy to point the finger, sometimes it is the other way around too. I believe without any doubt that sex is not often the problem.

You must get to the root of the problem before you can solve it, and the root of the problem with the majority of broken homes is lack of communication. People are so used to covering their true feelings lest they get hurt, that they bury what was the bud of a relationship and refuse to allow it to blossom.

That bud needs to be set free, released completely in order to receive the sunshine and nurturing needed. You cannot remain withdrawn like a turtle's head and expect to get anywhere, you'll never blossom. Communication must be a two-way relationship. You need to transmit and receive. When the bud received the words of love and encouragement needed, the bud will open up in a very beautiful natural way. **There is no life so broken that Jesus cannot restore it.**

We allow ourselves to be fed so much garbage, on television for example, that we lose touch with love inspired intimacy. Not lust filled intimacy, but the beautiful intimate moments a couple can have when they look to each other for their fulfillment as they talk freely and without any inhibitions. Allowing the love to blossom in a beautiful healthy way will result in two blossoms becoming a bouquet, Christ centered.

If more couples would just eliminate all the third objects that tend to put a wedge in their relationship, such as television programs that do the talking instead of the couples talking one on one, more couples would have stronger healthier relationships. Without these obstacles hindering their relationships, they would be free to communicate.

Eliminate the time you spend working, eating, reading the paper, watching television, cutting the grass, and ask yourself how many minutes do you spend on an average day in actually conversing with your family?

When you face the truth, you will find the answer you are searching for is right in front of you. Eliminate the mountain that gradually crept up on you and wedge their way between you and your spouse.

Then as you talk openly, there is but one more thing to do to have a victorious marriage. You must keep Jesus in the center and have your priorities in order, in GOD'S order. This is not "square" nor is it a lot of hogwash. It is the only answer and you know it deep in your spirit. But you have been afraid to try it.

The enemy has been holding you back because he does not want you to stop watching shows with no morals at all, semi-nude women, shows about the occult, depressing soap operas, gambling game shows, etc. He doesn't want you to be home with your family instead of at the sports arena with your buddies, or the race track or the hotels and dance halls.

Satan wants you to continue undressing every female you meet, with your eyes (and the same goes for the women undressing the men); but don't forget that God sees and knows all and He is the One who you will have to answer to someday.

Satan wants you to do your own thing; he keeps telling you this is the only way to be happy, by doing what you want when you want and how you want. But satan is a liar and a thief. The only way you will ever be free is when you get off the devil's highway and start trucking for Jesus, as I did! He is in the driver's seat, and it is a good thing. I simply do this, **"Where He leads me, I will follow."**

> *In almost two years of serving him, He has never led me anywhere I don't want to go and I've never been happier. Join me, on the highway to heaven, won't you? There's room!*

> *I just finished writing this chapter non-stop, and have not shed one tear. When I wrote in the beginning about feeling ashamed and embarrassed about things I did in the past, that was how I felt then but no more! That is sin that God forgave and replaced with His thoughts and a desire to live a holy life. FYI: No fishing. I am free. Hallelujah.*

God has given me inner healings that no psychiatrist could ever give me. God is the great healer. When we walk in the Spirit of God we will not fulfill the lust of the flesh. It is true, it is scriptural, and I know, because I have been walking side by side with the Lord and am not looking back.

That is the only reason that I have not fulfilled the lust of the flesh. I learned I am complete in Him; one is a whole number. How wonderful it is to know the Lord in such a personal way so that I can benefit fully from all that He has to offer. All of His gifts are on an accessible shelf, all we have to do is reach out, receive, and believe his Word as we walk with him hand in hand.

This does not mean that I never have a desire to have sexual relations. I am a human being with a healthy sexual appetite to be fulfilled within the confines of marriage. Meanwhile, there are certain things I try not to think about. This helps. I do my best to be led by the Holy Spirit so I will not be tempted by the lust of the flesh. Actually, crucifying the flesh is a daily necessity. It starts in the mind, which is the battleground.

(Jesus never married, and He never sinned, so don't say it is impossible.) Keeping my eyes on Jesus, thinking godly thoughts and not giving loose rein to my body is the answer. **1Cor.9:27 "But I keep under my body, and bring**

it unto subjection: lest that by any means, when I have preached to others, I myself should be a castaway."

I am complete in him. How wonderful to be free of bondage. It is a decision each individual must make, they can think about sex and they can choose to think about other things that will encourage them to walk in the Spirit. Once the right decision is made the rest is easy because the desire is gone and the Lord is right there to hold your hand and guide you.

I have been forgiven much, and I love the Lord very much. **Luke 7:47 "...Her sins, which are many, are forgiven; for she loved much: but to whom little is forgiven, the same loveth little."**

I am a virgin in the Lord and am extremely happy and give God all the glory because He taught me how to abide in the vine, and when there was temptation He has always provided a way of escape. As I came into the fullness the Holy Spirit encouraged me to take the godly route, and I did. Praise God for how merciful and loving He is! To forgive a sinner such as I, and then to use me for His glory is more than I can understand, but I do thank Him, and will follow Him wherever He leads me. My life has been converted in every sense of the Word and God did it all, through Jesus Christ, His only begotten Son. (John 3:16) **Don't ever give up because God can do anything! Believe it! I do!**

Only God could covert me, as He did and make me a vessel He can use for His glory. He did it for me and He is no respecter of persons. He'll do it for you. Give up the phoniness and start to live a fulfilling abundant life as you live for JESUS…He's the answer!

Psalm 18:43-50 (God's Word promising me that readers of this will bow to Him. Hallelujah!) "Thou hast delivered me from the strivings of the people; and thou hast made me the head of the heathen: a people whom I have not known shall serve me. As soon as they hear of me, they shall obey me: the strangers shall submit themselves unto me. The strangers shall fade away, and be afraid out of their close places. The Lord liveth; and blessed be my rock; and let the God of my salvation be exalted. It is God that avengeth me, and subdueth the people under me. He delivereth me from mine enemies: yea, thou liftest me up above those that rise up against

me: thou hast delivered me from the violent man. Therefore will I give thanks unto thee, O Lord, among the heathen, and sing praises unto thy name. Great deliverance giveth he to his king; and sheweth mercy to his anointed, to David, and to his Seed forevermore."

Frying Pan

This is a special poem
For the readers that cheat
And read the poem first
This time you will have to
Read the story first
As you should
I am sure the title
Has given you a thirst
To read each word
Because I took the time to write it
I sow seeds for Jesus and lift His Name
To God be the glory for lifting me
From the frying pan through the fire
To a gloriously happy end

An end to the old nature
A new beginning for me
As this rose is in full blossom

Will never wilt or fade
Because she is sees spiritually

She is not artificial
She is for real
As she lets her light shine
And serve God
With Spirit given zeal

Now read the story
I know you will be blessed
I was too
When I realized writing this story
Was the passing of another test
How wonderful it is
When God speaks through you
How can anyone help but love Him
When loving you...
Is all He desires to do.
You can't out love the Lord
I know. I tried.
But you can never love him too much either
Read the story please.
It is time you became His Bride!

CHAPTER 21

─── ❧ ───

Freedom

HERE I AM divorced, finally, with an unhappy marriage behind me, and anxious to being dating again as I did in the teenage years. I had my own idea of how things had changed, but I was a long way from the reality of 'dating today'.

After some weeks of attending meetings with single parents and visiting bars afterwards, getting a date was yet to be a reality. My girlfriend and I asked each other, **"Is this for real? People just don't date anymore, they simply meet somewhere, go home together and make love to each other, often never seeing each other again?"**

The more times we went out the more times we became desperate to have a proper date. Now there wasn't even a pretense of a date as the man bought dinner for two and theatre tickets, at least; then tried his so-called luck with his date, and it did not result in submission by many women even though they may have wanted to surrender. **They at least had some sense as to the value of their body, and cared how it was treated.**

NOW, there is not even a feeling of shame as total stranger meets, the spirit of lust overtakes, and they succumb to it. They do not consider their bodies sacred in any way.

From what I observed, most non-Christian women do not know how to get a guy without using their bodies. They thing they must use their bodies to compete with other women. For those that are overweight, they are often even more desperate. The slim pretty girls are with someone, but, what kind of a relationship is it?

A one night stand, and when he's gone, she cries her heart out because there is still a void that has not been filled! In most cases, yes, but few will admit to it. In all cases, actually, because you cannot fill a spiritual void with anything but Jesus, so the longing continues.

Other women go home without a man, feeling they lost out, yet, are already looking forward to the next night. The devil encourages them to return by telling them the next night will be their night to be with their "macho man" they are looking for.

What a phony, sad, desperate, lonely way to live! People who act more like animals than people. I know and can say this because I was one, and it is a living hell!

I had my freedom, I was a single again, with no pressures or ties, but I was not happy. I had what I thought I had wanted, but found out I must still have wanted something more, or I would have been happy already. That something more I needed was Jesus, and He is the answer for everyone else too.

I pray this poem "Freedom" quenches some desires the enemy has given you, because I learned the hard way the answer is not mankind, or booze, or anything else.

The answer is JESUS. Put him first in your life, and then the right marital relationship will follow, as the Holy Spirit inspires that relationship to blossom under the covering of God, and with God's blessing!

Freedom

Oh, to be single
Alone, and free
No ties, no pressures
Just freedom and me
Well, I've got my freedom
I'm single
I'm alone
But the freedom means nothing
Some think
When I sit
Alone........hoping
Hoping someone will drive by
Or call on the phone
A friend to talk to
So I won't be alone
But there are no phone calls
There are no dates
I'm popular and friendly
Attractive and without a mate

So what is the reason
I can't get a date
The guys I know
Are all friendly to me
We visit, we joke
We enjoy each other's company
Well I'm tired of trying
To figure it out
But there's one thing for sure
Without a doubt
If you are married
And wish you were free
Don't envy the single people
Like me
The grass is not greener
On the other side
I speak from experience
Because I have tried

CHAPTER 22

You Reap What You Sow

THE SOBER-FACED DOCTOR confirmed what I had suspected. I was absolutely mortified, I wanted to crawl away and just die. I felt like the lowest kind of animal there is. How could I ever face anyone! If was almost like I felt people would know what disease I had just by looking at my face. Expressions reveal much.

All I could think of was what I assumed was an old saying, "You reap what you sow." Little did I know then it is in the Bible. **Galatians 6:7-9 "Be not deceived; God is not mocked: for whatsoever a man soweth, that shall he also reap. For he that soweth to his flesh shall of the flesh reap corruption; but he that soweth to the Spirit shall of the Spirit reap life everlasting. And let us not be weary in well doing, for in due season we shall reap, if we faint not."**

I wondered why I thought this would never happen to me. Who did I think I was that I could play with fire and never get burned? It was like the neighbor that was killed in a car accident; you never think it will happen to anyone you know. Somehow it doesn't seem so bad if it is someone you don't know. Not in God's eyes though. A life is a life and He sent His Son that we may have eternal life.

John 3:16 "For God so loved the world, that he gave his only begotten Son, that whosoever believeth in him should not perish, but have everlasting life." Each life is very important to Him.

In my mind, I imagined all kinds of germs just multiplying as they ate away at my body. I felt like I was dying a slow death and since I was allergic to penicillin, I became even more concerned about whether or not medication would be effective. There was no way I could talk to anyone about this, that's for sure! (How ironic, to have felt as I did, and now be able to reveal all to so many. Romans 8:28 in action again, Praise God!"

Unfortunately, the doctor was of no assistance in this respect because he was so used to treating victims of venereal diseases that I could have had a headache and received the same degree of compassion.

When I told him, I would never get it again because I learned my lesson and sex was not worth risking this, (I was refer-ring to illicit sex, not sex between husband and wife), he was quite surprised at my attitude. He was of the casual attitude that this will be over with soon because it was caught in the very early stage so I was not to be so concerned. He said he wouldn't stop having sex because this happened to him. I was appalled!

God gave me the boldness needed to say a few things to the doctor at that time and I praise Him for it. Even in the sorrowful mess I was in, I was able to spread the Good News that I don't need sex anymore because I found what I'm looking for and it's not sex, it's Jesus!

The doctor handed me a pamphlet on VD that I was scared to read. He knew my fear but did not give me the comfort I needed by telling me more about this disease, which I really knew almost nothing about... that's why I was so afraid, it is the unknown that we often fear most.

I know when I'm not happy and the only difference between the doctor and I, is the fact that I admit it, and I do something about it. Actually, it wasn't what I was going to do, but what I WASN'T going to do that was the beginning of getting right with God. I was especially sure my days of having intercourse were over until I married. I just knew that I knew that God would help me to walk in the Spirit and not fulfill the lust of the flesh.

The doctor still had an expression of, **"Poor dear, giving up sex just because of this..."** on his face when I left, and I can't help but wonder if I looked like I couldn't believe he was actually serious.

After receiving a needle in the arm to take a blood test and an injection in the hip, I was even more determined to stay on the straight and narrow. Needles are something I have never taken a liking to, and don't expect I ever will. I was so exceptionally nervous that I jumped, causing the needle to go into the muscle. NOT funny at all!!!! The doctor's comment was so "Right on!" when he said, **"You shouldn't have done that."** Mind you, I knew that even before he said it because it was me on the receiving end of the pain when the needle hit deep on target. (I don't want to blame God for anything but I couldn't help but think of the words: "Lest we forget!" After all, He does have a good sense of humor.

The thing about this that made me feel so badly is the fact that this happened after I had made my decision to follow Jesus, and I have never had intercourse since being saved. I had contacted the disease unknowingly just before committing my life to the Lord. Consequently, I was heartbroken. This seemed so unfair, poor pity me. I had a good long pity party but it didn't do one bit of good because tears didn't wash away the problem. Although, on second thought, they did relieve the pressure.

As I sat at the kitchen table my chin resting on my hands, I had an experience I will never forget. **Jesus walked right through the wall, his hand extended... His face full of love.** I saw Him with spiritual eyes, a spiritual vision. Moments like this one cannot adequately be described. I can't tell you that I saw his face clearly, because I didn't. **I just knew it was Jesus and I was so sorry I had not reached out to Him earlier.** Self-pity and condemnation is the devil's way of keeping your eyes on self and off Jesus.

There were so many, many times in my life when I thought Jesus must be on the opposite side of the wall, but now I knew that He wasn't, because I had walked away from Him.

Now the joy of receiving divine help is something the devil sure can't give you. Only God had the perfect answer for me at that exact moment when I was shaken with fear over what must be happening to my insides. He knew better than I exactly what I needed and He met my need. He promises in **Philippians 4:19 "But my God shall supply all your need according to his riches in glory by Christ Jesus."**

I also learned how true it is, **"You reap what you sow."** I praise God because the problem was totally gone in a very short time, and I learned a lot from the experience. I also thank the Lord for delivering me from the bitterness I first experienced, and am grateful that even though I made a lot of mistakes, at least I didn't get angry at God because of this happening.

Deep within, I knew I had been guilty of sinning. No one forced me. I had a free will and there is no way around it. Bottom line, I was guilty, yet had been forgiven. However, I learned there would be repercussions. I did not need anyone to tell me. I knew and felt absolutely terrible. I prayed for healing and tried not to look back.

Will you accept the healing Jesus has for you now as you claim his promise in **1Peter 2:24 "Who his own self bare our sins in his own body on the tree, that we, being dead to sins, should live unto righteousness: by whose stripes ye were healed."**, or are you going to follow the accuser, the robber, the thief, the destroyer?

The decision is yours; but bear the following in mind, you will reap what you sow, without a doubt. Jesus does not lie and he promised in **John 10::10 "The thief cometh not, but for to steal, and to kill, and to destroy: I am come that they might have life, and that they might have it more abundantly." Romans 6:23 "For the wages of sin is death; but the gift of God is eternal life through Jesus Christ our Lord."** That is serious business, sin births spiritual death.

God is bigger than any problem you have, or think you have. He can pick you up. He wants you to keep your eyes off self and on Jesus. Sit on your pride, that's the best place for it, and listen as the Holy Spirit speaks to your heart (even the deaf can hear the voice of God because He speaks not to your ear, but your heart). Hallelujah. Allow Him to minister to you as you become still, and know you are in the presence of God.

Reach out now. You are precious in the sight of God so hold your head high and stand tall. No greater love hath anyone, than the love God has for you. You are never alone, He has been with you all the time and will not forsake you. Stop walking away from Him and start walking with him.

You Reap What You Sow

Floods of tears
Heart shattered
Body gradually shrinks
Germs spread like hells fire
Ultimate embarrassment
Desire of life extinguished
Severe withdrawal
Solitary confinement
Forced against the wall
No one I can talk to
My burden I cannot share
The guilt I feel envelops me
It is everywhere
There is only one place I can turn
But it is the best place of all
For Jesus has walked
Right through my wall

His hand is extended
His face full of love
Whatever...
Was I thinking of!
The JOY of receiving DIVINE help
Of knowing He's there all along
He was NOT on the opposite side of the wall.

Available Soon: 'Praise The Lord'
- Life AFTER The Cross
☺

www.ingramcontent.com/pod-product-compliance
Lightning Source LLC
Chambersburg PA
CBHW051820090426
42736CB00011B/1566